Modern Natural
Natural Modern

Modern
Natural
Natural
Modern

Houses

Ron Broadhurst
Foreword by Barry Bergdoll

RIZZOLI
NEW YORK

First published in the United States of America in 2010
by Rizzoli International Publications, Inc.
300 Park Avenue South, New York, NY 10010
www.rizzoliusa.com

2010 2011 2012 / 10 9 8 7 6 5 4 3 2 1

Printed in China

Design by Beatriz Cifuentes-Caballero

ISBN: 978-0-8478-3477-8

Library of Congress Control Number: 2010927878

Acknowledgments

Thank you to the architects and photographers whose brilliant work
fills these pages. My thanks also to Barry Bergdoll for his insightful
and elegant foreword.

At Rizzoli International Publications I am grateful to publisher
Charles Miers and associate publisher David Morton for
their enthusiastic support, and to editor Alexandra Tart for patiently
guiding this publication to completion. And I am deeply appreciative
of the support of Douglas Curran, Lynn Scrabis, and
Maria Pia Gramaglia.

I am also grateful to Taylor Yunis for his invaluable assistance
with translation.

Special thanks go to graphic designer Beatriz Cifuentes-Caballero
for her beautiful and intelligent work.

Contents

Foreword

Barry Bergdoll

Ever since Vitruvius made reference to the primitive hut as the origins of architecture, the single-family house has been both an archetype of the building art and the site for an exploration of the relationship humanity can forge between the natural world and the world of human constructs. Renewed at the dawn of the European Enlightenment of the eighteenth century, which established the parameters by which we still negotiate the natural and the technological, two influential theorists—the abbé Laugier in Paris and the rigorist Lodoli in Italy—changed the equation. Henceforth the primitive hut, with its manipulation of transformed tree trunks into shelter, was to be held up not as a distant reminder of how far architecture had progressed, but as a salutary reminder that architecture should never lose sight of the lessons of building in and with nature. The development of modernism in the twentieth century, with its embrace of new materials neither quarried nor felled—steel and other metals, concrete, and vast expanses of glass—posed new challenges to the ideals of a harmonic relationship between architecture and nature and at the same time opened up altogether unprecedented possibilities.

Of the broad spectrum of attitudes toward nature given form by modernist architects who most emphatically set the agenda and provided exemplars still referred to nearly a century later, the approaches of Frank Lloyd Wright and Ludwig Mies van der Rohe might seem the most definitively opposed. Throughout his long career Wright worked at honing and promoting what he called "organic" architecture. Organicism, for Wright, was a concept at once representational in his desire for a house that captured visually aspects of its site, an effort carried out in different forms and materials from the turn-of-the-century Prairie experiments to his final Usonian houses; and at the same time an abstract notion of developing the combinatory elements of an architecture from single repeatable elements that could be replicated and joined in complex ways—ways he believed paralleled the constructive laws of nature itself. Wright drew famously on his exposure—both as a child and through his wife's kindergarten teaching—to the Froebel block system, with its links of abstract form to natural processes. While a handful of the projects in this book follow the first aspect of Wright's concerns in the ways they allow the rhythms of the land to suggest a compositional strategy for a low-lying building, few engage with Wright's neo-Romantic belief that an architectural system itself can have the status of the building blocks of nature. This interest in an emulation of the systems rather than the forms of nature makes the work of Wright and his followers unexpected predecessors for today's digital research into biomimicry, where computer scripting has been allied to a fascination with what the last few generations of biological research has revealed about the codes of life in ecologies from the human body to the ecosystems with which we long to effect a new harmony. Much of the recent proliferation of writings on the return of nature has emphasized this world, in which complex systems of organization, as well as a sheer exuberant embrace of the ornament of pattern, has been heralded as a new embrace of nature in the potent world of digital tabulation and projection.

In the stunning panorama of contemporary work in single-family houses brought together in this volume, the world of biomimicry is largely absent; the aim, it seems, is to lay bare another tendency among up-and-coming practices worldwide to develop existential relationships to nature in a period when our formidable technological mastery shows us often to be at odds, if not even in open hostility, to nature. Here are to be found echoes of another line of twentieth-century research about architecture's relationship to nature—that embodied by Mies van der Rohe's residential work from the 1910s to the 1950s. But these concerns are now inflected toward a broader range of considerations, and respond often to a set of concerns and challenges that the heroic generations of modernists between the world wars or between World War II and the birth of the awareness of the ecological crisis in the late 1960s had only begun to imagine.

Mies van der Rohe's work has, in fact, rarely been associated with the natural. For many his intense, rigorous devotion to perfecting an abstract language of architectural space and materials, poised as a willing embrace of the artificial human nature of architecture, was a veritable anti-nature. But in the last decade Mies's designs and writings have been reconsidered as embodying a deeply committed relationship to nature, his commitments as much a matter of seeking an architecture that could provide a frame for a more profound daily experience of man's place both in and outside of nature, a relationship as more philosophical than mimetic. The white steel frame of the integrally glazed Farnsworth House (designed 1947), lifted (almost) above the flood plane of the Fox River in Illinois, creating thereby a transcendent floating world of architectonic perfection is a case in point. Mies here perfects themes he had been working on for a decade since arriving in Chicago and encountering American steel frame construction, which he was to rapidly endow with a language of full poetic mastery. But he also completes a decades-long treatment of the house as a platform both for the experience of nature and for the contemplation of the gaps that consciousness creates between us and the natural order of which we are such an ambiguous part. Mies himself said as much when he described the house as box-seat for experiencing the multiple acts of the annual drama of nature. The house's longest occupant, Lord Peter Palumbo, endorsed this from experience, explaining "Living in the house I have gradually become aware of a very special phenomenon: the man-made environment and the natural environment are here permitted to respond to, and to interact with, each other. While this may deviate from the dogma of Rousseau or the writings of Thoreau, the effect is essentially the same: that of being at once with Nature, in its broadest sense, and with oneself."[1]

Such an attitude is to be found in the vast majority of projects assembled here. All of the projects explore the duality between establishing an artistic frame in which the everyday is at once heightened and transformed and working with materials and construction methods to craft buildings of great integrity in and of themselves. It is this duality that recognizes that architecture is never directly a mimetic art, aping its context or naively deploying the materials directly at hand. The challenges to architectures of responsibility in a world of ecological fragility demand a complex calculus of materials and construction methods, and the algorithms of sustainability change with each context. Despite our globalizing world, what is appropriate in the outskirts of Mumbai or of Santiago de Chile can scarcely be the same, even if one of the achievements of this book is to offer a global survey. There is no direct representational link between an architecture that respects nature and crafts a place for us to cultivate that respect and the actual forms and materials of construction. No single dogma can respond at once to the demands of a fragile global ecology and the continued psychic value of respecting the genius loci. Architects set out to explore both the range of possibilities available in today's material palette—one whose ultimate sustainability has to do with complex calculations that cannot be reduced simply to the basic notion of a revival of local traditional practices in all situations—and to investigate anew what was present from the first dwelling, a need for an emotional and a philosophical, as well as a pragmatic, relationship between architecture and nature. This is an approach that is often transformative, but so too are the explorations of myriad other approaches that never lose sight of the necessity of renegotiating with each new project the potent possibilities of a dialogue between modernity and nature.

1 Lord Peter Palumbo, preface to Martiz Vandenberg, *Farnsworth House (Architecture in Detail)*. London: Phaidon, 2005, 7.

The Prism and the Cave

Ron Broadhurst

Perhaps the most iconic image of modernist architecture in concert with nature is that of Philip Johnson's Glass House crowning an idyllic New England hilltop. In fact, Johnson's refined, transparent pavilion, built in New Canaan, Connecticut, in 1949, is the mature expression of an inclination among earlier modernist architects to reconcile a technologically motivated, machine-age idiom with the beauty and satisfactions of the natural world. Along with Mies van der Rohe's Farnsworth House, completed in 1951, the Glass House could be considered the culmination of a tradition extending back at least as far as Le Corbusier's Villa Savoye, completed in 1931. Raised on slender white *pilotis* and surrounded by meadowland on all sides, the Villa Savoye itself was the final example of Le Corbusier's Purist architectural compositions; it was also designed and built concurrently with his Villa Mandrot, a prescient amalgam of modernist principles and primitivist impulses constructed of stone walls within a steel frame. But whether in the machine-age cave represented by the Villa Mandrot as well as by Le Corbusier's turf-roofed Petite Maison de Weekend of 1935, or in the pristine, dematerialized volume of the Glass House, the early material pliability of modernist ideals informs the range of approaches toward nature by the structures featured in this volume.

Of all these projects, the Square House, designed by Makoto Takei and Chie Nabeshima of the Japanese firm TNA, most closely adheres to the classic modernist ideal. A precisely square glass box elevated on slender white *pilotis*, the Square House seems at first glance to be the perfect twenty-first-century exemplar of both Miesian and Corbusian ideals, yet Takei and Nabeshima take a playful approach to the commission, giving the house a slightly sloping roof and clustering the *pilotis* so that they define the house's interior spaces in rows much like walls. The result is an array of slender pylons almost as irregular as the arrangement of trees on the house's sloping site.

The Square House demonstrates the quality that has allowed modernism to endure with such vitality into this century—its nearly infinite adaptability, as exemplified in Pezo von Ellrichshausen Architects' Casa Poli on the remote Chilean seacoast. Here Mauricio Pezo and Sofia von Ellrichshausen confidently adapted an earlier scheme for a house in a dense forest, Casa Rivo, where their primitivist/modernist monolith was executed in wood rather than the roughcast concrete of the later Casa Poli.

Cecilia Puga's House in Bahia Azul, also in Chile and also constructed of roughcast concrete, offers further evidence that a traditionally industrial building material need not be unsympathetic to a spectacular natural setting, as does Smiljan Radic's Pite House, which has the added dimension of a poetic garden of sculpted stone on its breathtaking rooftop entry platform. Alejandro Aravena's Pirihueico House maintains a similarly poetic quality, being conceived as a response to the client's request for a house "the color of shadows." The result is an earthy yet elegant essay in stone and wood. And wood construction distinguishes the Kiltro House by Juan Pablo Corvalan of Supersudaka, a "mongrel" amalgam of projects by Le Corbusier, Mies van der Rohe, Rem Koolhaas, and even fellow Chilean Smiljan Radic.

The fact that Radic, Corvalan, Aravena, Puga, and Pezo and von Ellrichshausen all work in Chile points to a strain of regionalism running throughout this book. While the evidence for any theory around what lies behind the "new Chilean architecture" would be purely anecdotal here, it is safe to suggest that the rich qualities of the country's seacoast and mountains have contributed to the proliferation of first-rate projects that fit perfectly within the rubric of houses that are either composed of natural materials or maintain an engaging relationship to the natural landscape, or both.

Similarly, the presence of a significant number of Swiss projects in these pages can be largely attributed to the inspiration these architects derived from a series of spectacular sites. Add to this a rich vernacular building tradition and a robust appreciation for modernist ideals, and one has a recipe for some of the most ambitious essays in natural construction materials and finishes featured in this volume. Also impressive is the variety of expression for these projects. Compare the two ski chalets featured here: EM2N's Mountain Chalet is distinguished by its open, dormitory-like spaces and rough-and-ready interior finishes, while Andreas Fuhrimann and Gabrielle Hächler's House on the Rigi achieves a level of refinement far exceeding that of a conventional chalet.

Of the three projects located among lower-lying Alpine hillside sites, Laurent Savioz and Claude Fabrizzi's Maison Germanier is unique as an example of adaptive reuse, occupying the shell of a house dating from the mid-nineteenth century. However, the local stone construction technique employed for the Maison Germanier is also the guiding principle behind the structure of the House in Brione by Markus Wespi and Jérôme de Meuron. Here Wespi and de Meuron took an innovative approach—treating the creation of built space as a subtractive process—to a traditional material; they also relieved the stark geometry and blank walls of the house's exterior profile with large perforated wooden doors, another gesture toward the local building vernacular. For the Villa Vals, in a celebrated Swiss spa town, Dutch architect Bjarne Mastenbroek of the firm SeARCH and Swiss architect Christian Müller have taken the concept of architecture as a subtractive process to a dazzling degree that the architects themselves characterize as being "slightly absurd."

The country represented here with the greatest number of featured houses is Japan. But unlike the Chilean and Swiss architects, whose projects embrace or even defer to their stunning landscapes, these Japan-based architects often have negotiated a more complex relationship with a context that may be urban or suburban, and in some cases they have created projects that interrogate the very

Glass House, New Canaan, Connecticut © Ezra Stoller/Esto

Maison de Weekend, La Celle-Saint-Cloud, France © FLC/ADAGP

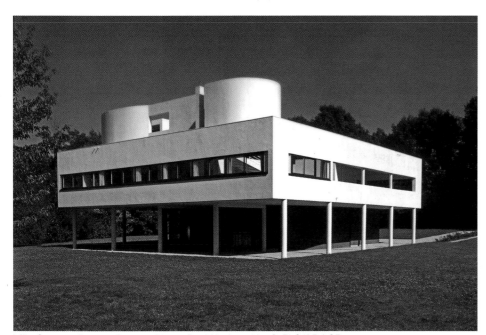

Villa Savoye, Poissy, France   Photo Paul Koslowski   © FLC/ADAGP

idea of a "natural" condition. Hiroshi Nakamura of NAP Architects faced the rare opportunity of building on a heavily wooded plot in the heart of Tokyo, taking pains to preserve as many of the existing trees as possible, even going so far as to wrap elements of the structure around individual trunks. Conversely, Makoto Tanijiri of Suppose Design Office was charged with providing a "garden room" for a house on an impossibly narrow site in the center of Nagoya, where he wound an indoor, rock-filled, planted corridor along the perimeter of the house and around its glass-enclosed living spaces. Sou Fujimoto orchestrated a similar intervention of natural elements into an urban site, this time in Utsunomiya, just north of Tokyo. Here Fujimoto planted an array of trees on top of and among a disjointed agglomeration of white cubes, each containing a room and together comprising a 660-square-foot house. The result straddles the futuristic and the primitive.

The protean Fujimoto also designed the 7/2 House, which in these pages signals a departure from the Japanese urban center. The elongated, saw-toothed profile of the wood-clad structure playfully echoes its hilly landscape. A similarly simple structure designed by Go Hasegawa reveals hidden complexities within its seemingly naïve single-gable volume. Hasegawa's House in a Forest is one of four houses in this book that are located in the resort town of Karuizawa as part of an ambitious development project composed of formally bold weekend homes including Kotaro Ide's Shell House and another project by the architects of the Square House, leading this discussion back in circular fashion to Makoto Takei and Chie Nabeshima of TNA, whose technically virtuosic Passage House itself exists in circular fashion.

The remaining project located in Japan, Atelier Bow-Wow's Izu House, represents a response to a considerably more straightforward set of conditions: a sloping seaside site that was formerly a tangerine plantation. However, even here architects Yoshiharu Tsukamoto and Momoyo Kaijima took the opportunity to exercise their signature combination of playfulness and intelligence to create a wood-framed light construction that is formally inventive while always oriented to the special qualities of its site. A project by one final Japan-based architect, Kengo Kuma, is featured in this volume, though the house, called the Great (Bamboo) Wall, is located in China, not Japan. Long enamored with delicate and attenuated structural elements, Kuma chose bamboo as the dominant finish for the house, not only for its material lightness but also for its local symbolic significance as a historic export from China to Japan.

Even more acute local significance informed Studio Mumbai's design for the Palmyra House, nestled within a coconut plantation an hour outside of Mumbai and distinguished by copious louvers fashioned from the region's abundant palmyra tree as well as local ain wood for the house's structural frame. Similarly, KieranTimberlake's Loblolly House takes its name from its site's abundant loblolly pines, which are echoed by the irregularly placed timber pylons supporting the elevated structure.

The three featured projects located in Scandinavia are all informed by local conditions or customs to one degree or another. Swedish architects Bolle Tham and Martin Videgård stained their elegant Archipelago House, constructed of fir plywood, to emulate the Baltic Sea, which it faces from its idyllic island site. Norwegian architects Einar Jarmund and Håkon Vigsnæs sourced building materials to an extremely local degree, cladding the Farm House with timber from an adjacent century-old barn, while Håkon Matre Aasarød and Erlend Blakstad Haffner of the firm Fantastic Norway found inspiration for their wooden Cabin Vardehaugen in traditional Norwegian "cluster structures."

Both the Farm House and Cabin Vardehaugen ambitiously employ passive methods of energy conservation, with the Farm House acting as a giant solar heat collector and Cabin Vardehaugen functioning as a self-enveloping windbreak. But among the architects whose work is featured here, it is Australian architect Sean Godsell who is perhaps most dedicated to the ideal of sustainability. His austere and sleek Glenburn House is one in an impressive line of essays in sustainability undertaken since Godsell established his own practice in 1994.

While the Farm House, Cabin Vardehaugen, and Glenburn House work as machines for energy conservation, Rocha Tombal's Bierings House and Allied Works' Dutchess County Guest House function purely as idealized sculptural objects within their respective contexts: banal and suburban for the Bierings House, sylvan and virtually pristine for the Dutchess County Guest House. The hardest work these thoroughbreds do is frame their occupants' experience of the world beyond their walls, either by way of whimsical, contorted dormers as in the Bierings House or by the literal frames that wind their way around the Dutchess County Guest House. And it is fitting that the latter occupies an idyllic site like its twentieth-century progenitors, a polished, decidedly twenty-first-century composition of organic and inorganic materials in harmony with the wilderness.

House in Bahia Azul

House in Bahia Azul

Cecilia Puga
Bahia Azul, Chile
2002

Chilean architect Cecilia Puga found inspiration for this seaside weekend retreat in a highly unlikely source: the common sight of abandoned railway stations in the north of Chile. The clients intended to host their large, multigenerational family for holiday getaways, so Puga's first decision was to separate the basic functions of sleeping, eating, and gathering as much as possible by assigning each to its own pavilion, whose elongated form would recall simple rural railway station houses or the container cars on a railway line. The intention was to create a cluster of closely gathered but structurally independent volumes that would manage to maximize both proximity and privacy.

Axonometric drawings

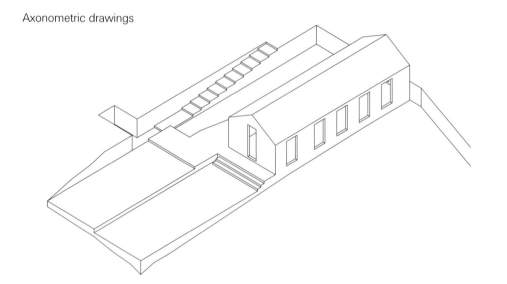

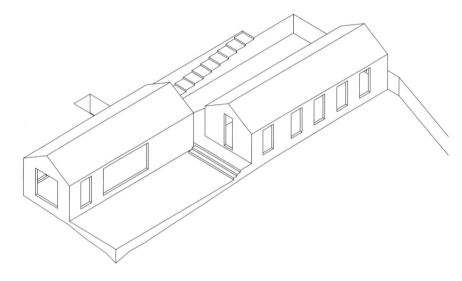

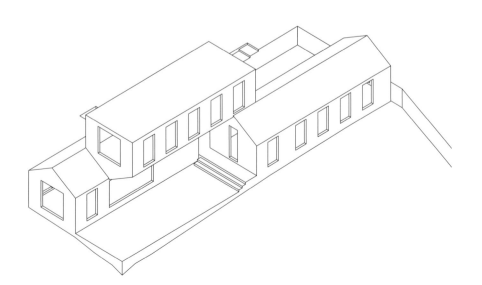

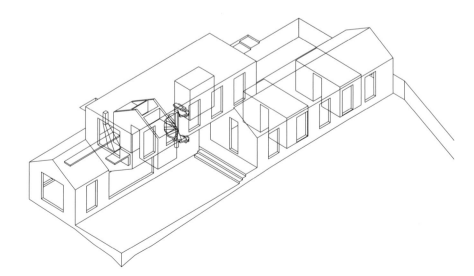

Once Puga made the initial decision to separate programmatic functions in this manner, her next major decision was to excavate the site as close to the point at which the plot dropped into the sea as was reasonably possible. From there it became clear that the optimal arrangement of the house's main volumes, all executed in roughcast reinforced concrete, would involve stacking. The abstract notion of separate rectangular pavilions then began to take on the shape of three simple peaked-roof house forms, one of which—containing the main living space and the master bedroom—would be inverted and stacked ever so nimbly on the corners of the other two, the first of which contains an open kitchen and dining space as well as a spiral staircase up to the living volume, and the second of which contains a dormitory-style sequence of sleeping spaces that open onto one another in a manner not unlike a series of railroad cars.

Cross sections

Plans

Architect Cecilia Puga found inspiration for this seaside weekend retreat in the abandoned railway stations in the north of Chile. Puga's intention was to create a cluster of closely gathered but structurally independent volumes that would maximize both proximity and privacy.

Following pages: Puga situated the house as close to the point at which the plot dropped into the sea as was reasonably possible, taking full advantage of the house's spectacular setting.

Opposite and top right: The open dining space and kitchen maintain the same roughcast reinforced concrete materiality as the exterior.

Bottom right: The living room occupies the house's upper volume, where it provides a contemplative perch from which to survey the surrounding seascape.

Mountain Chalet

Mountain Chalet

EM2N Architects
Flumserberg, Switzerland
2003

For this weekend ski retreat, Swiss architects Mathias Müller and Daniel Niggli of EM2N concentrated on the qualities of the spectacular mountainside site to create a distinctive house on a relatively modest budget. The point of generation for their design was a rejection of the idea of a weekend house as simply a conventional luxury villa executed at a smaller scale.
The architects' first gesture was to site the structure close to the adjacent ski slope to emphasize its role as a temporary station for recreation rather than a full-scale house. Visitors can ski right up to the fir-clad structure, whose towerlike proportions reinforce its ski-station profile.

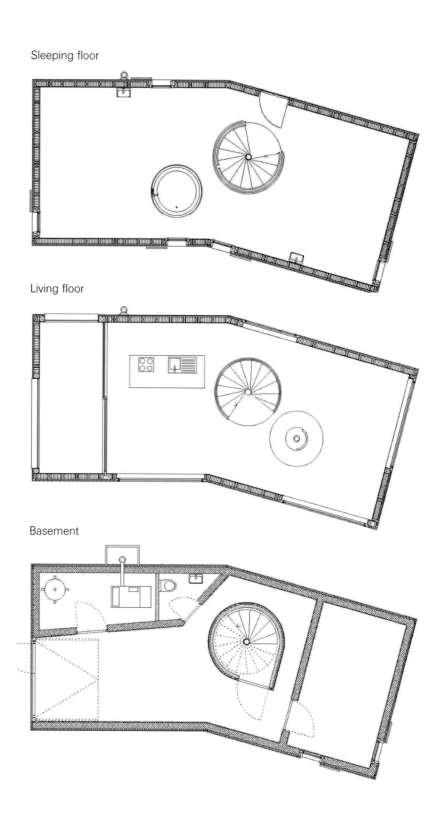

Sleeping floor

Living floor

Basement

For the interior spaces the architects were inspired by the idea of a one-room house, or dormitory, so they placed two simple open spaces on top of each other, and on top of a concrete, ground-floor garage level required by zoning laws. The lower-level sleeping area can accommodate up to eight people in an open space broken up only by the spiral staircase that links all three floors and by a freestanding bathtub. Two sinks punctuate either end of this chamber dedicated to *existenzminimum*. The house's upper level contains an open living space that is fitted out with a small kitchen and a podlike fireplace suspended from a slightly peaked ceiling, two simple elements that provide a great deal of domestic comfort in this context.

As with everything else, interior finishes and other details were determined by the constraints of the project's budget. Windows on the sleeping level were designed to be exceedingly small to allow for more generous expanses of glass on the living level. The interior of the basement level is lined with drain mats, an ingenious use of an unexpected material that gives the space an insulated, cavelike quality. The interior spaces of the two main levels are paneled in particleboard, another very inexpensive material, but one that lends the otherwise austere spaces a welcome touch of texture and warmth.

Southeast elevation

Northeast elevation

Section

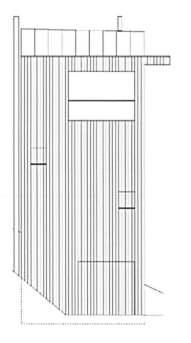

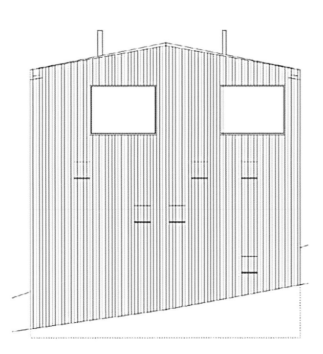

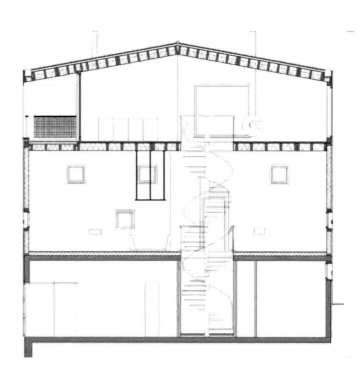

Opposite: Architects Mathias Müller and Daniel Niggli of EM2N sited the house as close to the adjacent ski slope as possible to emphasize its role as a temporary station for recreation rather than a full-scale house.

Right: The fir-clad structure's towerlike proportions reinforce its ski-station profile.

The lower-level sleeping space can accommodate up to eight people in an open space broken up only by the spiral staircase that links all three floors and by a freestanding bathtub.

Opposite: The house's upper level contains an open living space that is fitted out with a small kitchen and a podlike fireplace suspended from a slightly peaked ceiling.

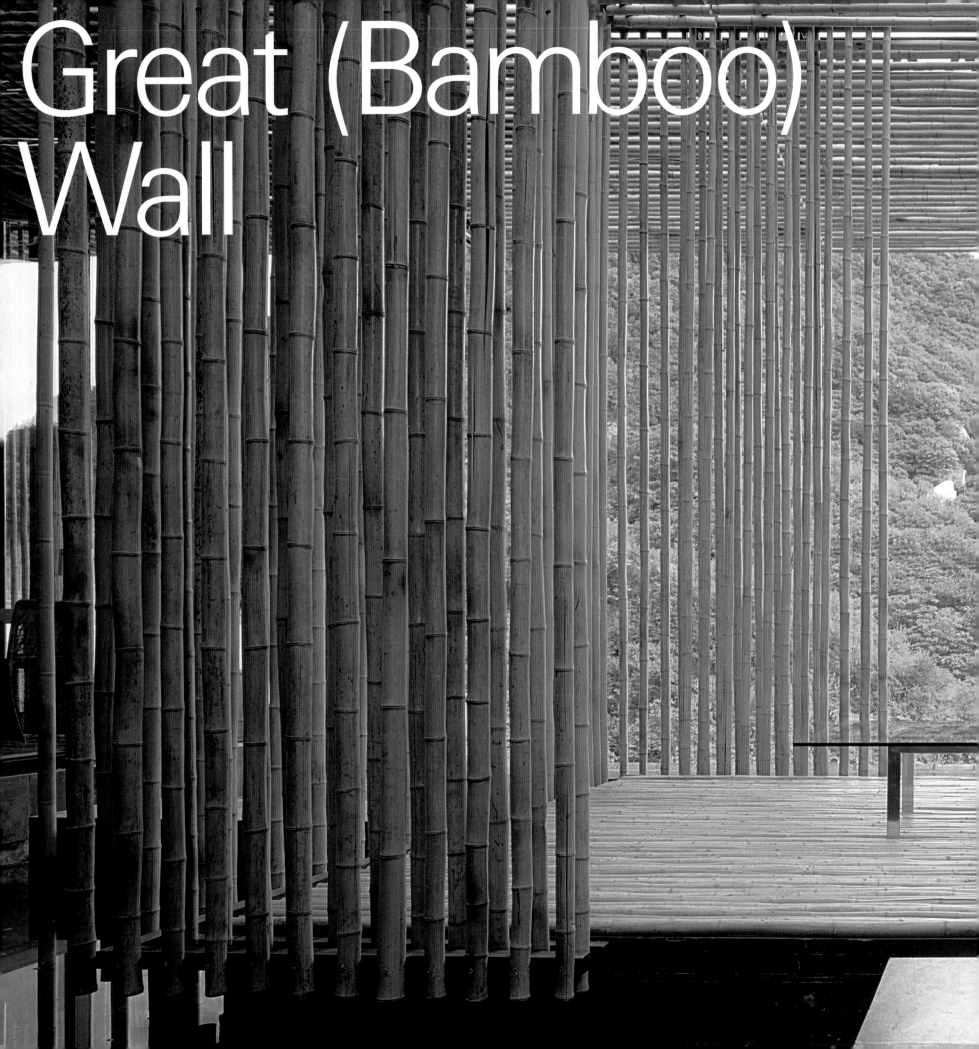

Great (Bamboo) Wall

Great (Bamboo) Wall

Kengo Kuma
Beijing, China
2003

Since the 1990s Japanese architect Kengo Kuma has endeavored to achieve what he has described as an architecture of fragmentation, in contrast to the heavy reinforced-concrete monumentality that characterized fashionable Japanese architecture in the 1970s and '80s. Over the course of the past two decades Kuma's light touch has distinguished his buildings for fashion juggernaut LVMH's Japanese headquarters in Osaka, stores for Lucien Pellat-Finet in Tokyo and Osaka, the Tiffany & Co. store in Tokyo's Ginza district, and numerous museums throughout Japan. The same delicate use of materials such as glass and attenuated wooden and concrete louvers in these projects also characterizes his scheme for the Great (Bamboo) Wall, a five-thousand-square-foot house located outside of Beijing on a rustic site near a length of China's famed Great Wall.

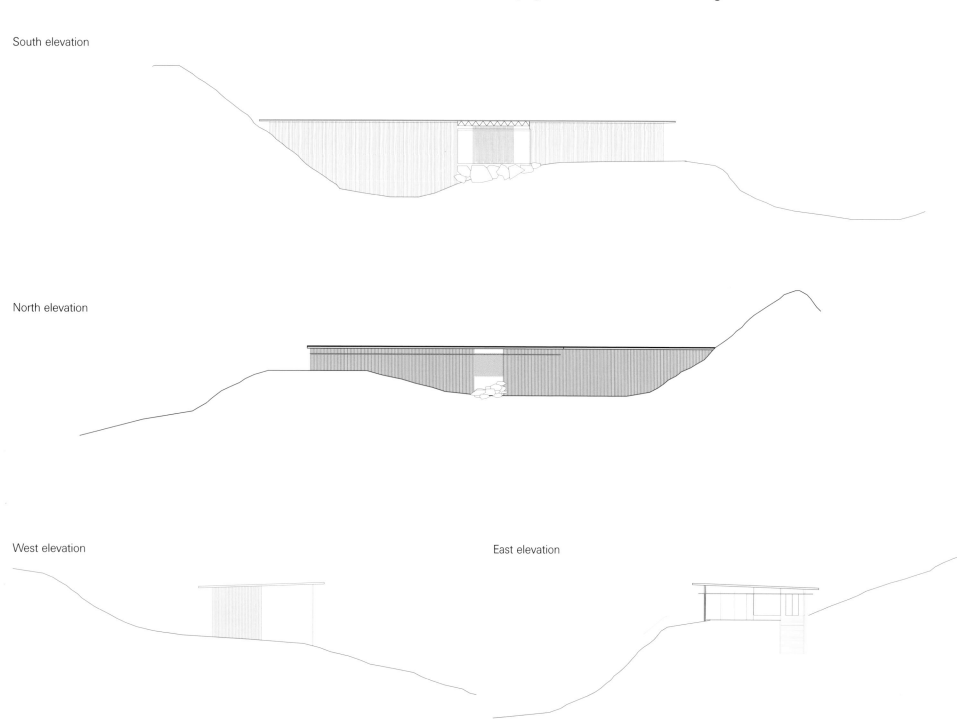

South elevation

North elevation

West elevation

East elevation

The house was commissioned as part of an ambitious speculative development in which ten Asian architects would ultimately design ten houses each. From the start Kuma wanted to create a house that was integrated with the hillside site, so to that end he took the adjacent Great Wall as a guiding metaphor for a house that would nestle half-hidden into the hillside like a wall. Bamboo was chosen as the house's predominant material finish for its transparency and delicacy—qualities on which Kuma has long placed a premium—as well as for its symbolic value as a historically significant export from China to Japan.

The rooms are arranged on two levels, with the lower level containing two bedrooms, servants' quarters, and mechanical and service spaces. The larger upper level contains four bedrooms and a grand, open, split-level living/dining space and kitchen. The black slate used on the floors throughout the dwelling takes on a spectacular effect in this showcase space and in the luxuriously proportioned entrance corridor, with its ceremonial staircase down to the secondary level. All of these public spaces are arranged around a square reflecting pool at the center of which is placed a sort of bamboo cage, accessed by two freestanding bridges seemingly floating like upended minimalist monoliths, where one can appreciate the beauty of both house and landscape in near absolute serenity.

Plan

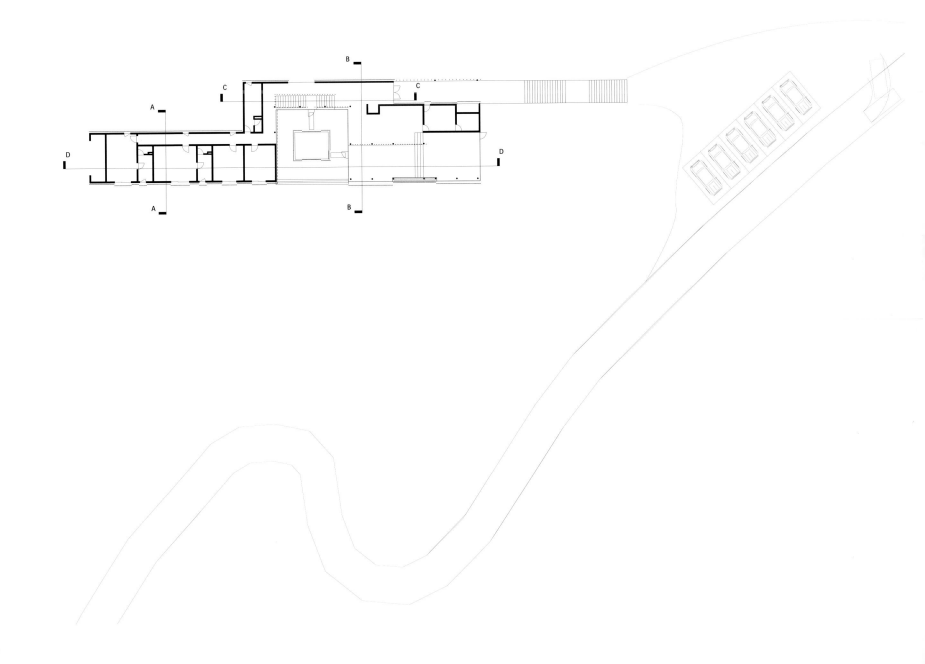

Opposite: Japanese architect Kengo Kuma's Great (Bamboo) Wall is a five-thousand-square-foot house located outside of Beijing on a rustic site near a length of China's famed Great Wall. Kuma took the adjacent Great Wall as a guiding metaphor for a house that would nestle half-hidden into the hillside like a wall.

Above right: Bamboo was chosen as the house's predominant material finish for its transparency and delicacy as well as for its symbolic value as a historically significant export from China to Japan.

Previous pages: The kitchen, raised a half level above the adjacent dining room, is distinguished by the black slate floors and bamboo-clad ceilings found throughout the house.

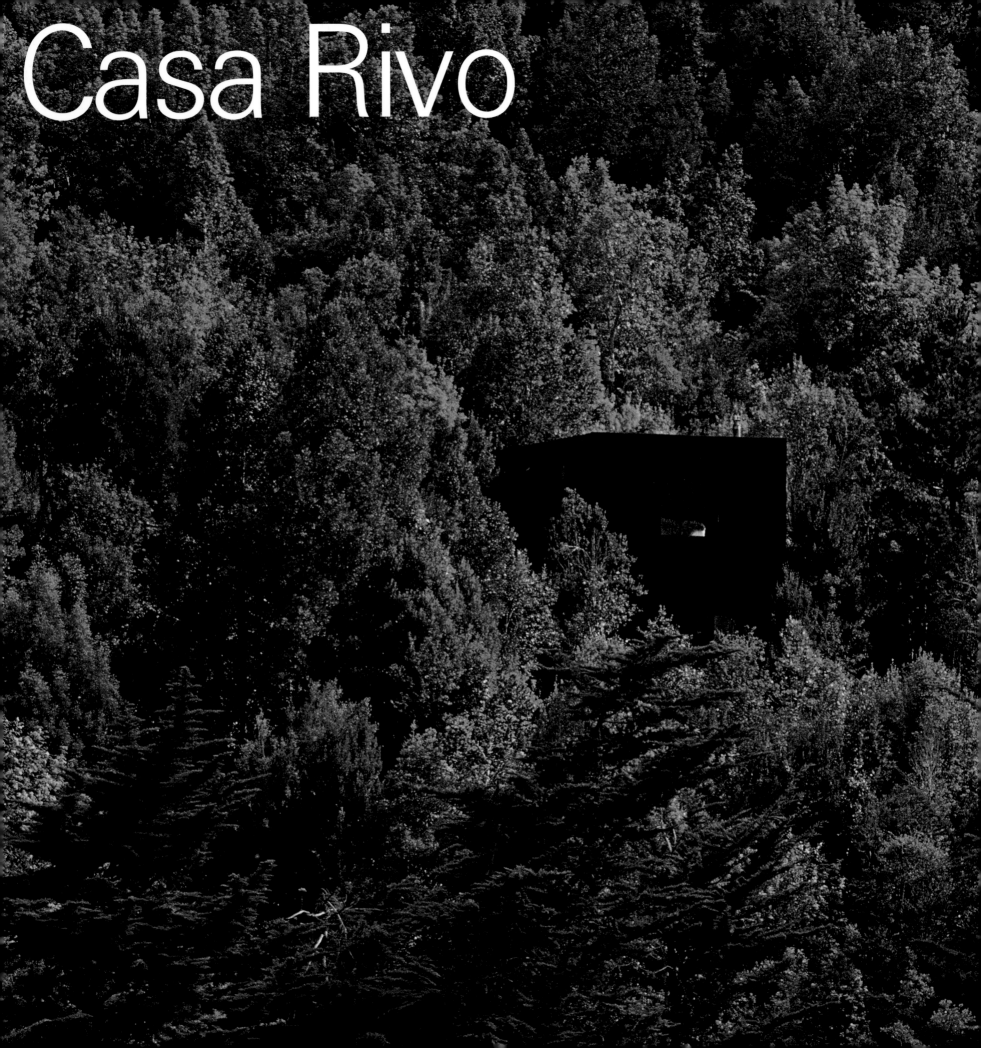

Casa Rivo

Casa Rivo

Pezo von Ellrichshausen Architects
Valdivia, Chile
2003

Casa Rivo, located in the dense forestland outside the southern Chilean city of Valdivia, is the first of a pair of houses designed by Mauricio Pezo and Sofia von Ellrichshausen that employ to good effect closely related spatial strategies for projects with highly differentiated programs, sites, and materials. The second, Casa Poli, on the following pages, is located on the remote, rocky, southern Chilean seacoast, and was designed with a decidedly public component to its program. Casa Rivo, however, required the architects to address the concerns their clients shared about being constantly together in such an isolated locale.

Axonometric

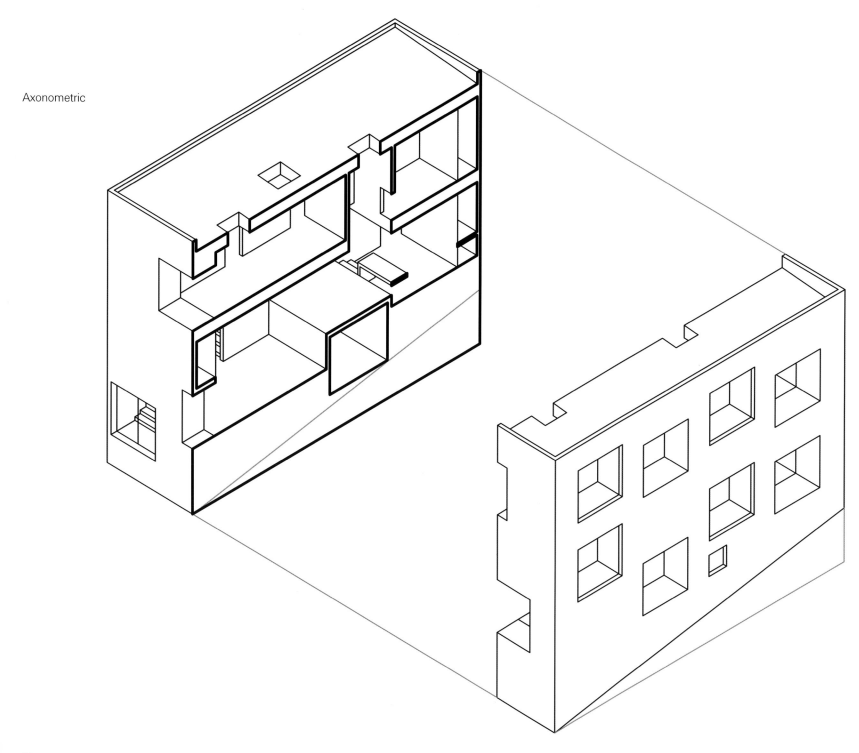

This worry on the part of their clients became for the architects the critical problem that informed all other formal decisions: first, to create a compact, monolithic volume that would feature panoramic views over the site's endless treetops from its upper levels; second, to create a system of thick, hollowed-out perimeter walls that contain stairs and closets and improve thermal insulation; and finally to place the greatest distance possible between the lower-level studio and the upper-level bedroom and office while unifying all parts of the house with a central living space.

The result is a simple cubic volume composed entirely of pine, with the exterior completely surfaced in untreated pine boards that were then coated in a mixture of oil and tar typically used in local barn construction. Inside this deceptively simple form is virtually a Chinese box of alternately interlocking and hidden rooms, corridors, and stairways. Inside, pine boards or panels face every surface—wall, floor, and ceiling—unifying the complex series of spaces with one another and with the epic rusticity of the house's deep forest setting.

Roof plan

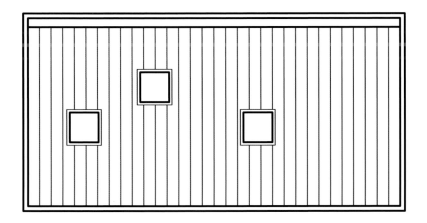

Second floor

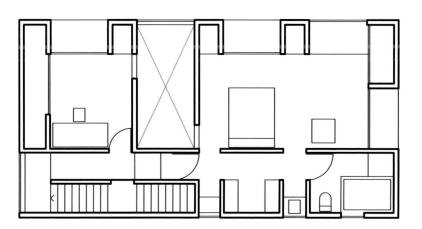

First floor

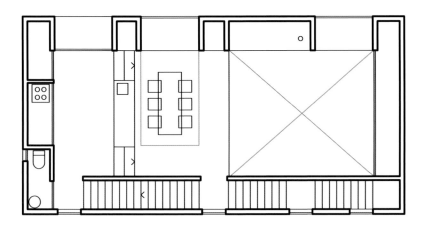

Ground floor

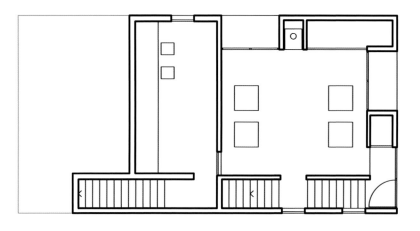

Opposite: Casa Rivo's simple cubic volume is composed entirely of pine, with the exterior completely surfaced in untreated pine boards that were then coated in a mixture of oil and tar typically used in local barn construction.

Right: Inside, pine boards or panels face every wall, floor, and ceiling (top). The interior spaces comprise a virtual Chinese box of rooms, corridors, and stairways (bottom).

Casa Poli

Casa Poli

Pezo von Ellrichshausen Architects
Concepción, Chile
2005

Located on the Coliumo Peninsula, a rural setting sparsely populated by farmers, fishermen, and the occasional summer tourist, Casa Poli was conceived as a compact and autonomous volume crowning its sublime clifftop site as if it were a natural podium. The program required that the building function as both a summer house and a small art gallery and performance space. So unlike the architect's earlier Casa Rivo, on the previous pages, where privacy was the paramount motivation for every architectural gesture, the interior here had to mediate between maintaining a highly public aspect and one that was intimate and informal, with a scale that would be both monumental and domestic.

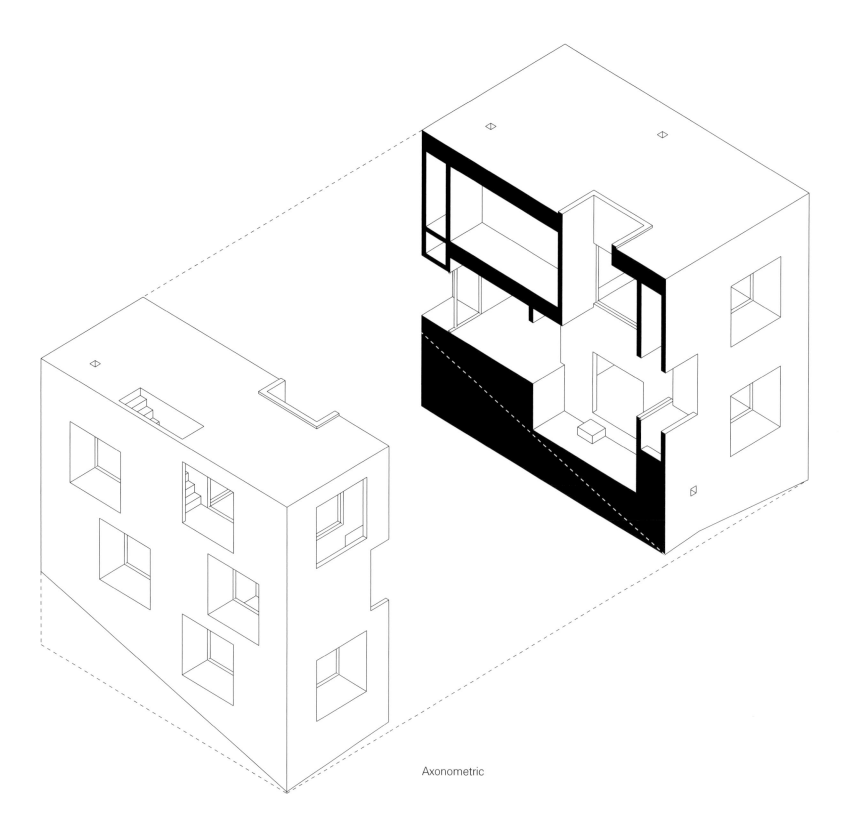

Axonometric

Such a multivalent program led the architects to create a series of interior spaces whose functions would remain indeterminate and flexible. To maximize this flexibility, all service elements—including kitchen, bathrooms, stairways, and closets—have been located within deep walls along the project's perimeter, exactly as in Casa Rivo. These perimeter volumes also house interior balconies that can serve as storage space for all domestic accoutrements, completely freeing the main interior spaces for social and cultural functions.

A simple material palette of handmade concrete formed with untreated, battered wooden frames gives the building's modernist profile a richly primitive and highly tactile quality that imitates the straightforward pine-board construction of Casa Rivo. The wooden frames used for the concrete formwork were also later used as interior door and window frames and in the construction of sliding panels concealing the various perimeter service elements and contributing even more to the house's primitivist/modernist character.

Ground floor

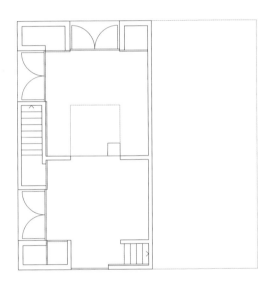

First floor

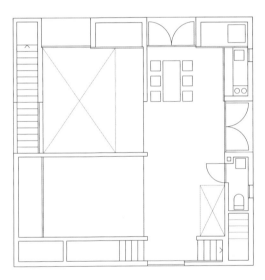

Second floor

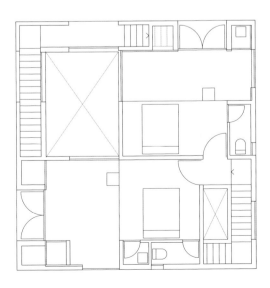

Roof terrace

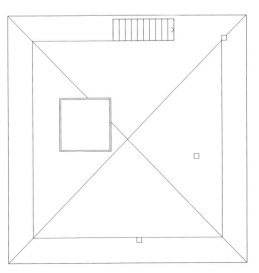

Opposite: Architects Mauricio Pezo and Sofia von Ellrichshausen conceived Casa Poli as a compact cubic volume crowning its cliff-top site on Chile's sparsely populated Coliumo Peninsula.

Right: The house's cubic form is punctuated by perfectly square apertures on all sides in a seemingly random fashion that gives each facade a unique profile.

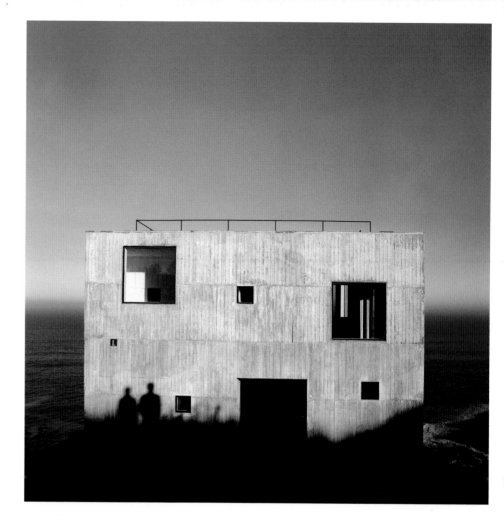

Opposite: Interior spaces flow openly into one another and around a central atrium space.

Right: The house's program called for a small gallery and performance space as well as a summerhouse, requiring the architects to design a series of spaces that would be indeterminate and flexible.

Opposite: The central atrium and the variety of window placement create an array of sources for natural light and views.

Right: A simple material palette of handmade concrete formed with untreated, battered wooden frames gives the building's modernist profile a richly primitive and highly tactile quality.

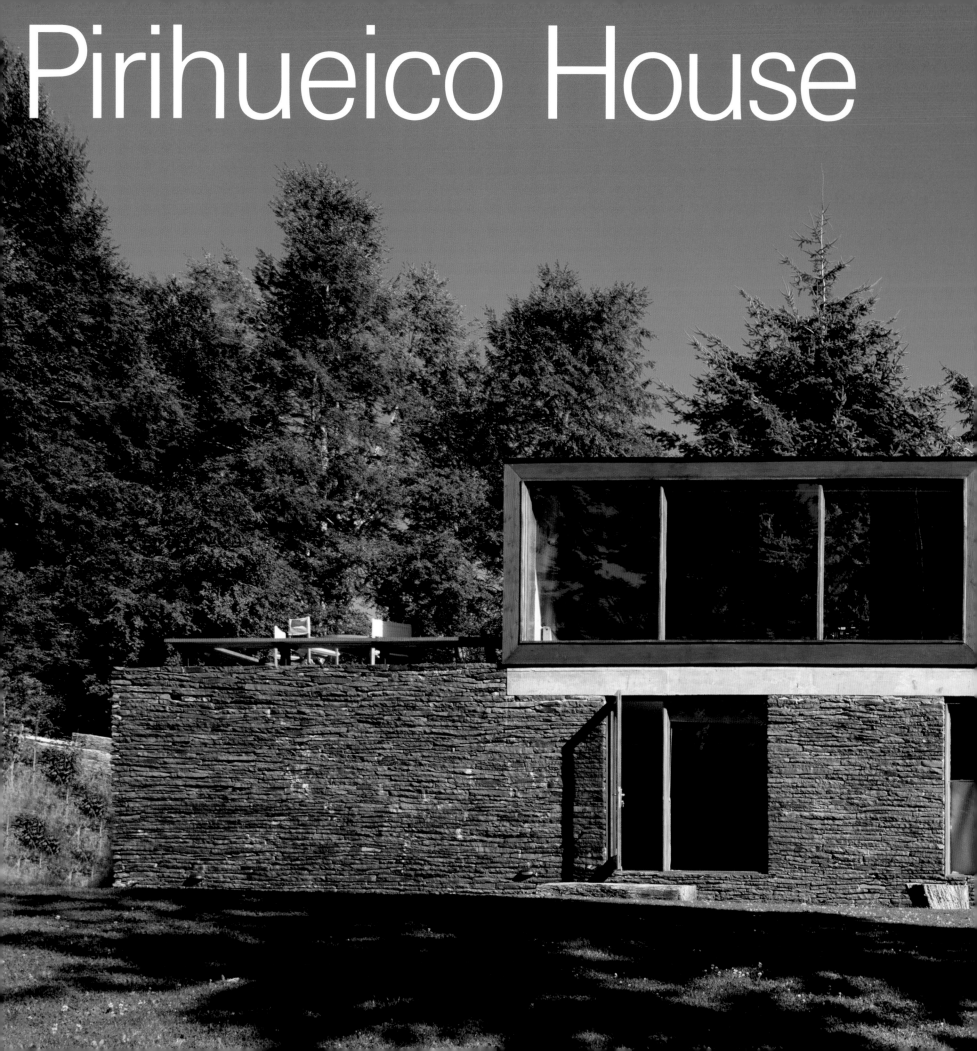

Pirihueico House

Pirihueico House

Alejandro Aravena
Pirihueico Lake, Chile
2004

Although Chilean architect Alejandro Aravena prefers to focus his energy on projects with some meaningful social component to their program, such as low-income housing or institutional work including buildings for the departments of medicine and mathematics at the Universidad Católica de Chile, he was intrigued by the request from the client of this 3,800-square-foot villa for a house "the color of shadows." Additionally, the house's location offered another set of intriguing challenges: situated in southern Chile, its forested site was distinguished by its extreme remoteness and heavy winds and rains throughout the year.

First floor

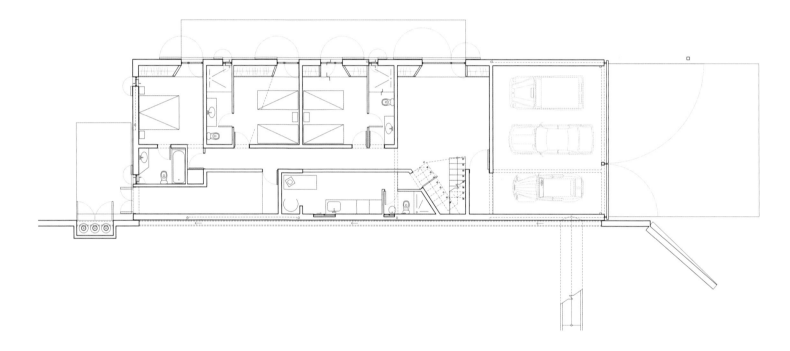

Second floor

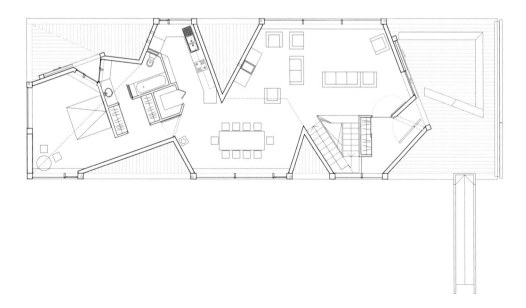

Aravena immediately began thinking of his design for the house as a response to the site's extreme conditions. Starting with a simple rectangular box capped by a conventional peaked roof, Aravena placed the main living spaces—composed of living and dining spaces, kitchen, and master bedroom—on the upper level and began to distort the scheme to take advantage of particular views or to offer maximum protection from the elements. Windows were extended upward to frame vertical elements such as trees or a distant forest path in dramatic fashion, while views of the adjacent volcanic lake inspired long horizontal glazing. And the resulting plan pivots and slices the interior spaces to create a satisfyingly complex suite of rooms.

The isolation of the site drove Aravena's placement of the main living spaces on a stone plinthlike ground-floor level—containing the secondary bedrooms and service spaces—whose rugged, sparsely permeated walls offer a great sense of security. The wood upper level then emerges as a highly sculptural yet formally subtle series of folded roof planes and irregularly framed expanses of glass. And together the stained wood of the upper level and the local gray flat stones of the ground level delivered to the client his house of shadows.

West elevation

North elevation

East elevation

South elevation

Right: The house's isolated site inspired architect Alejandro Aravena to arrange the main living spaces over a stone plinthlike ground-floor level that contains the secondary bedrooms and service spaces.

Opposite: The wood upper level is a highly sculptural series of folded roof planes and irregularly framed expanses of glass.

The main living spaces on the upper level take advantage of particular views, with windows that have been extended upward to frame vertical elements such as trees or a distant forest path, as in the kitchen (left), or horizontally to frame views of the adjacent volcanic lake, as in the living room (opposite).

Following pages: The stained wood of the house's upper level and the gray flat stones of the ground level together realize the client's request for a house "the color of shadows."

Izu House

Izu House

Atelier Bow-Wow
Nishiizu, Japan
2004

Since being founded in 1992 by Yoshiharu Tsukamoto and Momoyo Kaijima, Tokyo-based architecture firm Atelier Bow-Wow has built an international reputation for projects that are deeply informed by intensive research interrogating the most basic assumptions about building types. The firm's sympathies lead it to projects with modest budgets and an abandonment of conventional formal concerns in favor of a theoretical playfulness that pushes the definition of its work toward conceptual art. A review of the photography of its residential projects reveals spaces that are characterized by exposed wood studs and desultory furnishings, giving the viewer a sense of energetic messiness. While conceived at a larger scale than Bow-Wow's typical residential commissions, the Izu House is no exception to these principles.

Section

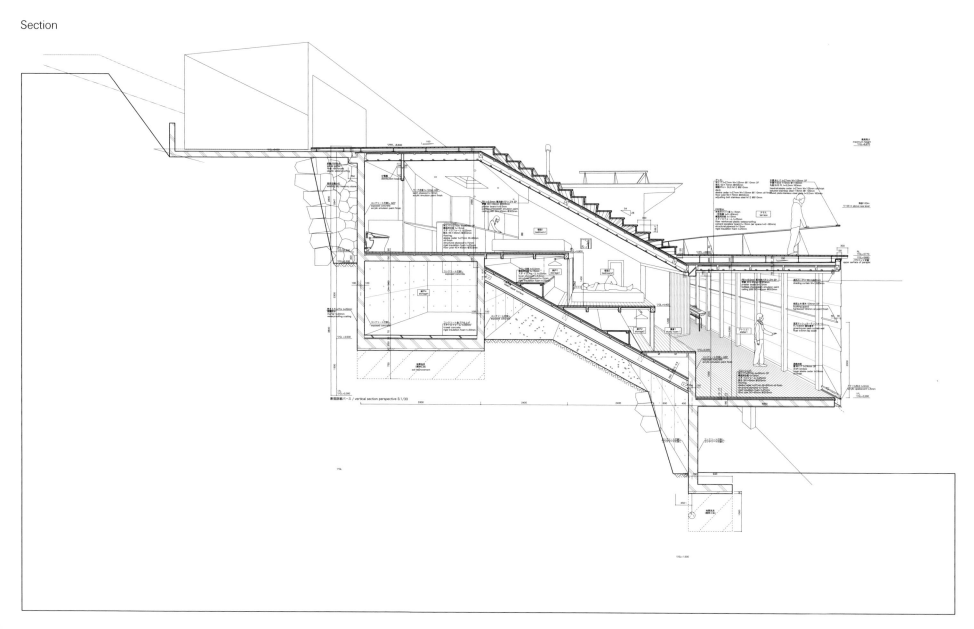

Sited on the slopes of a former tangerine plantation on the rugged coastline of Suruga Bay, on the Pacific Ocean, the Izu House is entered by way of the rooftop from an entrance road behind the house. A wide staircase leads down to the first of two living levels, which contains open living, dining, and kitchen spaces. These public living spaces pivot around the house's interior staircase, whose knotted wood treads cascade down the site's sloping ground plane to the lower floor, interrupted by large landings that function as open sleeping areas.

The high-ceilinged studio on the lower level bends along the contours of the site and showcases the house's light construction, with floor-to-ceiling glazing supported by sticklike wooden structural members. This structural lightness is expressed throughout the house, whether in the thin plywood panels on the more enclosed elevations or the delicate railing that lines the rooftop terraces and staircase. The overall effect is a structure, like all of Bow-Wow's oeuvre, that eschews any particular style for the qualities of lightness, openness, and utility.

Upper floor

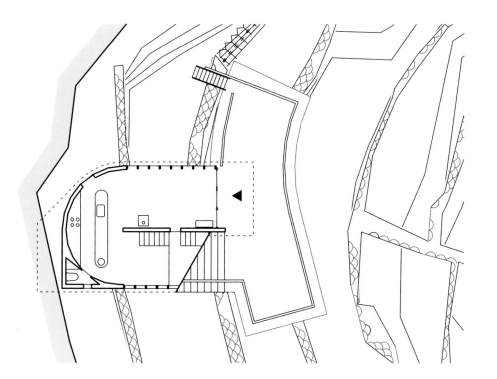

Lower floor

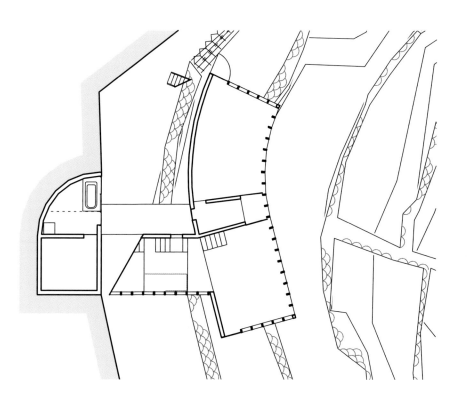

Opposite: Izu House, sited on a seaside tangerine plantation, is accessed by a wide rooftop staircase that leads down to the first of two living levels, containing open living, dining, and kitchen spaces.

Right: The living and dining space opens completely to the expansive terrace over the house's lower level, enjoying views of Japan's Suruga Bay on the Pacific Ocean.

Opposite: An interior staircase cascades down to a high-ceilinged studio on the house's lower level.

Left: The stairs are interrupted by large landings that function as open sleeping areas.

House on the Rigi

House on the Rigi

Andreas Fuhrimann and Gabrielle Hächler
Scheidegg, Switzerland
2004

Over the course of their relatively young careers, Swiss architects Andreas Fuhrimann and Gabrielle Hächler have consistently demonstrated a talent for adapting enduring Alpine building forms to the twenty-first century with a muscular yet restrained modernist sensibility. For a weekend house on the slopes of Mount Rigi in central Switzerland, Fuhrimann and Hächler revivified the simple form of the conventional ski chalet, retaining its straightforward wood construction and sloping roof but warping it into a diamondlike polygon shape.

Upper floor

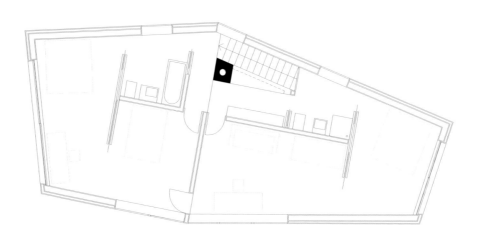

Middle floor

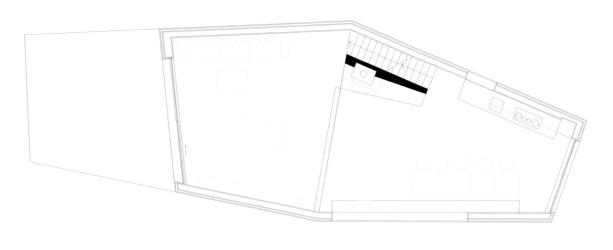

Lower floor

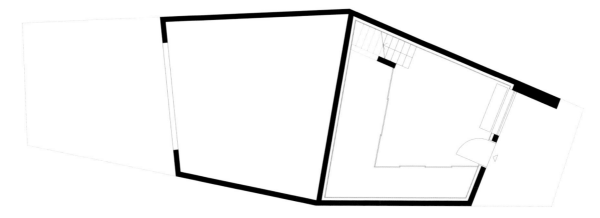

Anchored to the sloping site by a concrete basement/entry level, the wooden house emerges from the landscape in a manner that the architects compare to a ship coursing through a swell. This analogy led them to express the chimney top as a thin, elegantly articulated smokestack. The light, nautical formal vocabulary belies the solidity of the sculptural concrete fireplace on the first floor, which forms the focal point of the open living, dining, and kitchen space while operating as a structural nexus around which a simple staircase with open wood treads connects all three levels of the house.

The house's topmost level contains three bedrooms plus a study with sleeping accommodation, all arranged in a fluid plan that offers the trapezoidal rooms easy access to one another via wide sliding panels. The open living space on the main level is distinguished by the careful framing of the breathtaking views with a wall of sliding glass panels accessing an unobstructed terrace platform. An elegantly proportioned five-meter-long plate-glass window flawlessly frames the Alpine vista to achieve maximum visual drama.

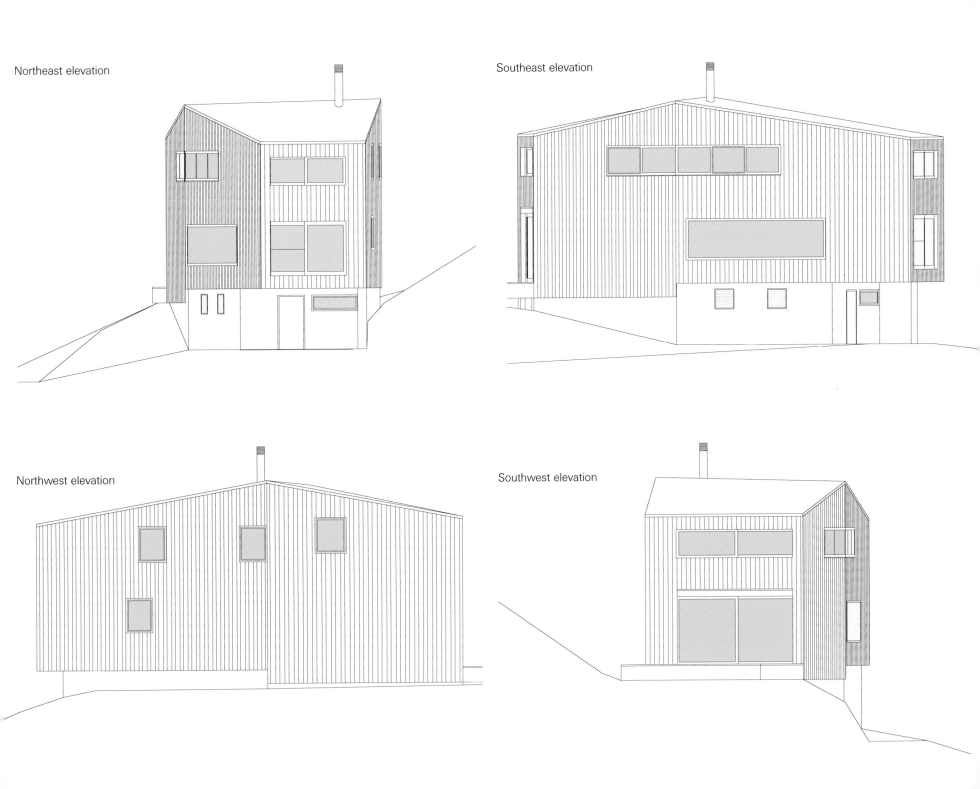

Northeast elevation

Southeast elevation

Northwest elevation

Southwest elevation

Left: The House on the Rigi sits perched on its mountainside site with a simple open terrace off the living room offering direct access to the surrounding slopes.

Opposite: Architects Andreas Fuhrimann and Gabrielle Hächler were inspired by the simple ski chalet for this wooden house set on the spectacular slopes of Switzerland's Mount Rigi, retaining its straightforward wood construction and sloping roof but warping it into a diamondlike polygon shape.

Following pages: The house's intriguing shape is countered by straightforward wood construction.

Opposite: In the main level's open dining space, an elegantly proportioned five-meter-long plate-glass window frames the Alpine vista to achieve maximum visual drama.
Right: A sculptural concrete fireplace forms the focal point of the open living, dining, and kitchen space.

Previous pages: The dining area is serviced by a simple kitchen counter, at left, leaving generous space for gathering and entertaining.

Pite House

Pite House

Smiljan Radic
Papudo, Chile
2005

The bold use of large-scale natural stone has become something of a leitmotif in the work of Chilean architect Smiljan Radic. Frequently collaborating with sculptor Marcela Correa, Radic allows his architectural projects to take on the qualities of highly lyrical tableaux in which the monumental yet desultory presence of Correa's stone interventions is simultaneously primordial and classical in character. Perhaps Radic's most ambitious use of stone has been in a park-side restaurant in Santiago where boulders support the roof like formless caryatids. For this 4,300-square-foot villa on the rugged Chilean seacoast, Radic again introduced Correa's stone sculpture to dramatic effect, this time by creating a mysterious garden of stone on the rooftop entrance platform of the hidden house.

Plan

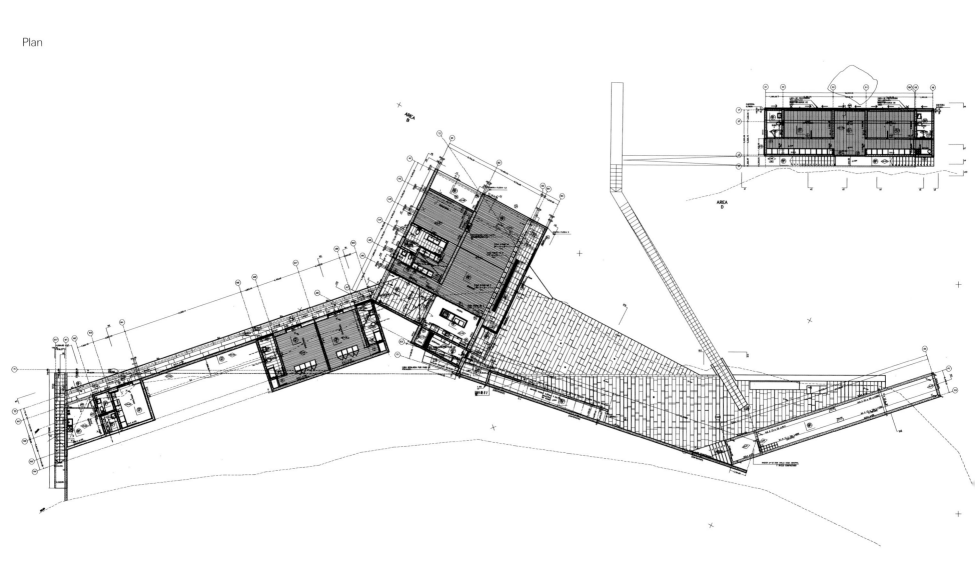

From this austere point of entry a ramp leads down to the sprawling house, which is an atomized collection of indoor and outdoor spaces oriented toward the sea. In addition to the main house proper, Radic has designed an extensive terrace accommodating an aggressively linear lap pool that seems to lunge into the ocean and a separate guest pavilion that is nestled at the bottom of the site on the rocky shore.

Within the house, the glass-enclosed main volume contains the open kitchen and living/dining space as well as the master bedroom, which enjoys a vertiginous view of the ocean. An impressive freestanding shelf unit spans the entire length of the open living and dining space, adding a layer of depth between these spaces and the vast entrance terrace. From this main volume pivots an outdoor, cliff-side corridor that accesses two additional bedrooms and, down an exceedingly long stretch, a private suite of bedrooms and bathrooms for staff. Extensive use of wood finishes characterizes the interior spaces, including wood floors, ceilings, and walls, depending on the room. Outsized wooden frames surround the windows and sliding glass panels as well as the large-scale pivoting glass doors that access the bedrooms from the precariously sited outdoor corridor. The overall effect is of a rustic yet luxurious villa that maintains an intensely poetic relationship to the surrounding landscape.

Elevations

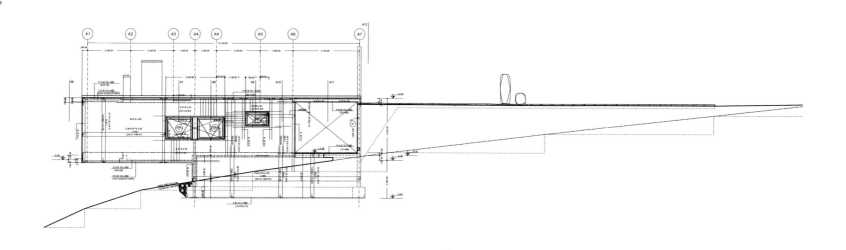

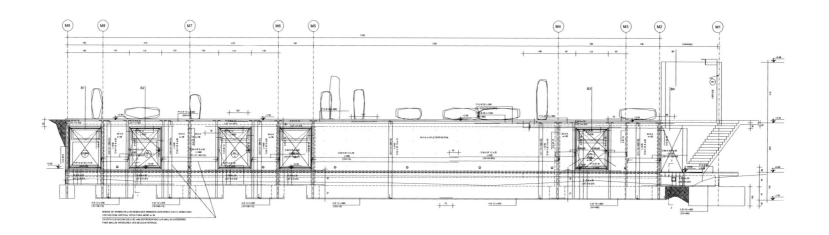

Left: From a stone garden on a rooftop entrance platform, a series of ramps leads down to the sprawling house and onto a separate guest pavilion.

Top right: A dramatic cliffside corridor accesses two bedrooms and a separate suite for staff.

Bottom right: In contrast to the main house, the guest pavilion, which comprises two large bedrooms and a central living room, offers a fully transparent, attenuated profile toward the sea.

Following pages: The ramp down to the expansive terrace creates a drama-filled entrance path to the glass-enclosed entrance gallery and main living space.

Left: The terrace accommodates a lap pool that seems to lunge into the ocean. Opposite: Stairways lead to the guest pavilion, which is nestled at the bottom of the site on the rocky shore.

Following pages: The main living and dining space is given a degree of privacy from the entrance gallery by way of a freestanding shelf unit, at right.

Opposite: Vertiginous ocean views
distinguish the master bedroom (top) and
the living room (bottom).

Right: An outdoor dining space connects
the house's main living volume to the open,
cliffside corridor.

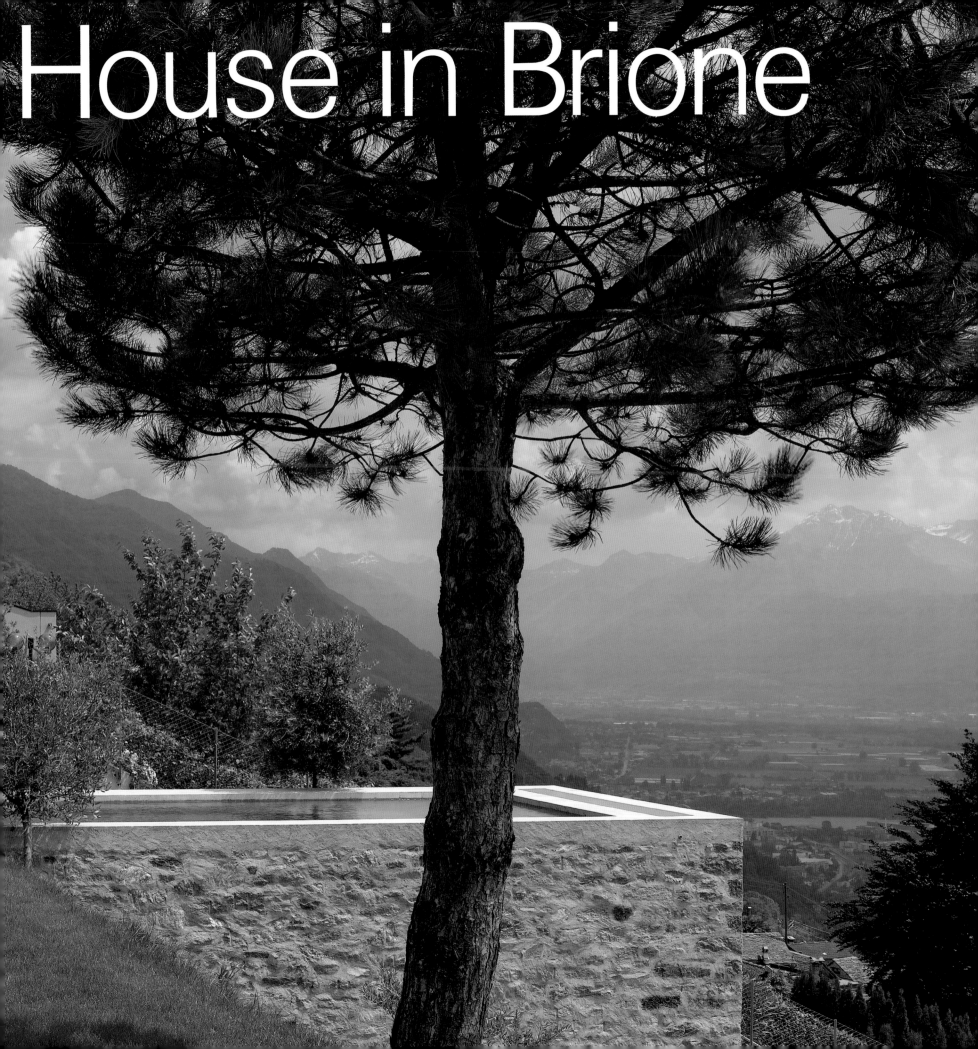

House in Brione

House in Brione

Wespi de Meuron
Brione, Switzerland
2005

This small weekend house located above Locarno, Switzerland, emerges out of its hillside site as two highly rusticated stone volumes. With both volumes backed up against the hillside site, the structure adopts the profile of a habitable wall, or a cave dwelling, rather than a house. In this spirit, architects Markus Wespi and Jérôme de Meuron approached the creation of interior space as a subtractive rather than an additive process.

First floor

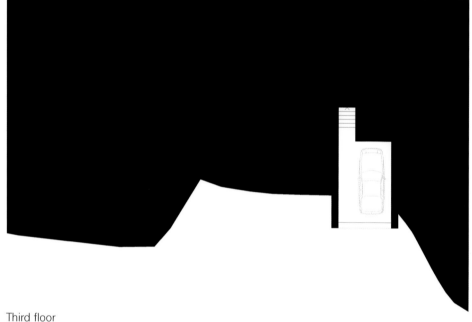

Second floor

Third floor

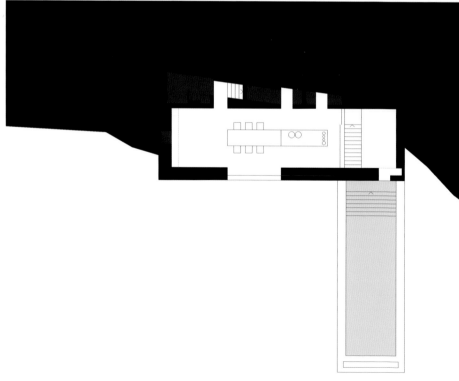

Fourth floor

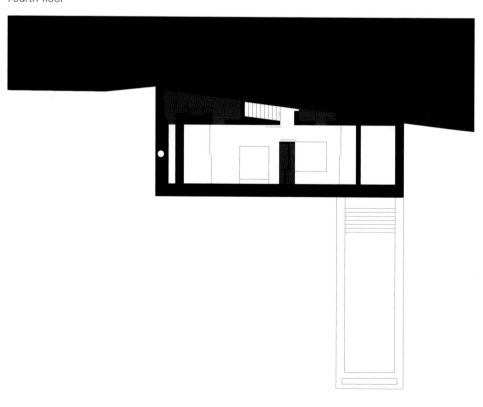

The lower volume contains a swimming pool that is accessed directly from the upper volume, comprising the house's two main living levels. Beneath the swimming pool, the architects have tucked a carport, which also serves as the main entry to the house. A narrow aperture along the pool's edge telescopes down to the carport, permitting almost monastic natural illumination. Two flights of stairs lead up to the main living level, which is organized around a long island counter that accommodates both food preparation and dining.

At the landing of the stairs from the carport, a double-height outdoor foyer, or courtyard, leads directly into the swimming pool through a narrow door. This small courtyard and another similar outdoor space on the upper level provide ample natural illumination to the house, which from the exterior takes on a nearly impermeable, fortress-like aspect. The hermetic profile of the house is relieved only by the presence of two large perforated wooden panels—one that is the door of the carport, and one that opens up from the main living space—which, along with the stone construction, acknowledges the region's building traditions.

Sections

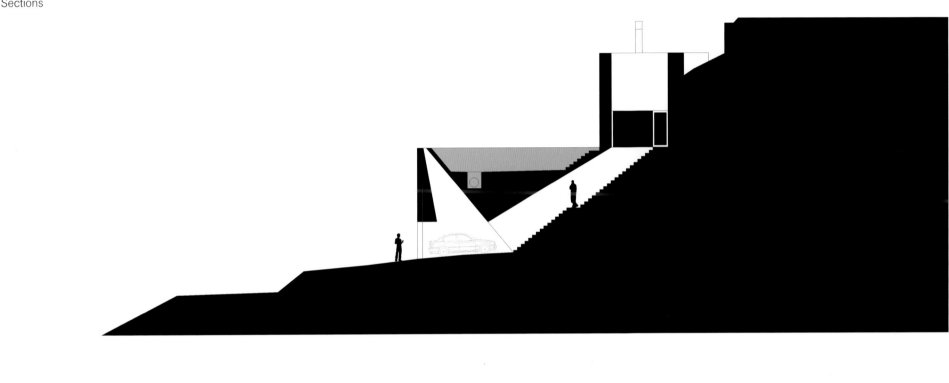

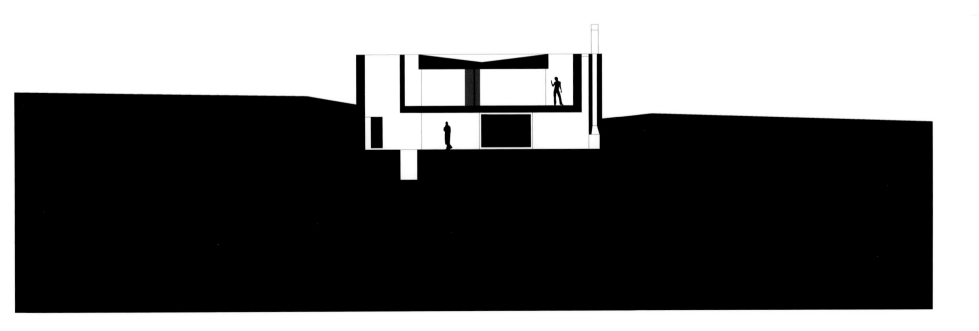

Opposite: On the house's front facade a large, perforated wooden panel opens from the main living space. Directly underneath the swimming pool the architects have tucked the main entry and carport.

Right: A double-height courtyard leads directly into the swimming pool through a narrow door.

Opposite: Under the swimming pool, the carport serves as the main entry to the house by way of a narrow double-flight staircase. An aperture along the pool's edge telescopes down to the carport.

Right: The house's fortresslike exterior is relieved by courtyards and skylights illuminating the interior.

Following pages: At the center of the main living space is a streamlined and simple kitchen island and built-in dining table.

Opposite: Both bedrooms offer access to a private courtyard, which provides a feeling of openness.

Right: Though completely concealed from the outside views, the master bedroom maintains a sense of spaciousness and warmth.

7/2 House

7/2 House

Sou Fujimoto
Hokkaido, Japan
2006

Japanese architect Sou Fujimoto maintains a protean approach to the design of houses, accessing a seemingly endless variety of solutions over the course of his relatively young career. The designer of two wildly different projects featured in this volume (see also his House Before House), Fujomoto creates houses that bear little formal relationship to one another and in fact appear to be so materially distinct that one wonders if Fujimoto is deliberately challenging himself to master every building material available to him, all the while displaying a dazzling degree of formal inventiveness.

Diagram

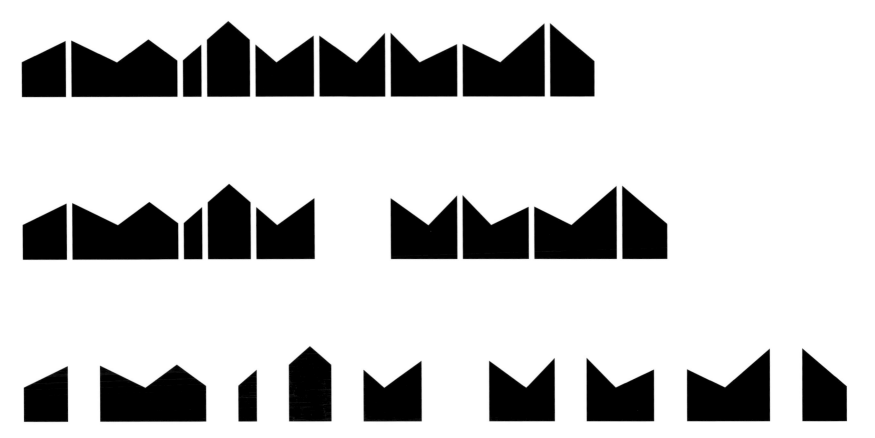

In the case of the 7/2 House, which is actually composed of two small, attached dwellings, Fujimoto fused together a series of seven simple wood-clad, peaked-roof house forms. However, since the number of spaces inside the structure does not correspond to the number of peaked-roof components, the interior spaces reveal themselves to have half-gable or multiple-gable ceilings, lending them an unexpected sawtooth quality.

Each dwelling unit comprises two compact bedrooms flanking an entry foyer and an open living/dining and kitchen space. The total area for both units is only 1,100 square feet, and the railroad-car order of the spaces achieves maximum efficiency. This simple arrangement is distinguished by the fitful, expressionistic angularity of the rooms' ceilings, which are punctuated by skylights, and by the extensive use of knotty wood flooring, which offers a warm, textural contrast to the house's stark, white walls that are only occasionally perforated by perfect-square apertures that open to the outside as well as to the adjacent rooms.

Plan

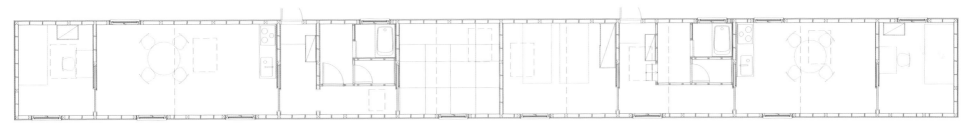

Section

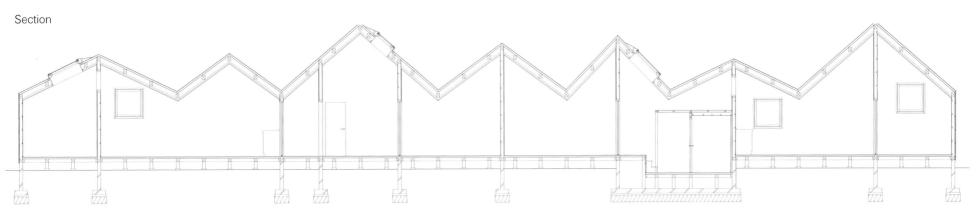

7/2 House is in fact composed of two attached dwellings, each comprising an open living/dining and kitchen space (opposite, left), an entry foyer (opposite, right), and two bedrooms.

Right: Perfect square apertures open to the outside as well as to the adjacent rooms.

Following pages: The deceptively simple form of the house, a string of gables, echoes the contours of Hokkaido's hilly terrain.

House in a Forest

House in a Forest

Go Hasegawa
Karuizawa, Japan
2006

Architect Go Hasegawa's design for a vacation house near the resort town of Karuizawa was deeply informed by its site. Nestled between a hillside boardwalk on one side and a quaint stream on the other, the site inspired Hasegawa to create a simple, single-gabled cabin in the woods, in this case so simple that it resembles a child's idea of what a house should look like. However, the house's exterior form belies a delightfully complex arrangement of interior spaces, each with its own gabled ceiling, making the simple cabin in the woods a secret agglomeration of peak-roofed spaces all collected within a single gabled "envelope" structure.

Plan

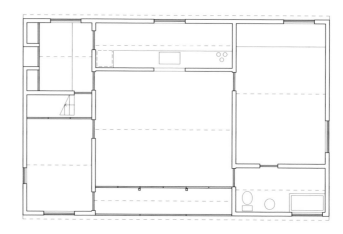

Roof plan

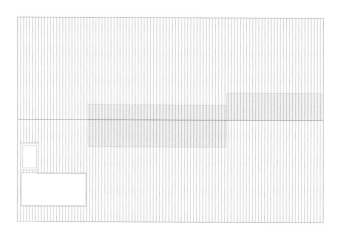

Each of the interior spaces, including a living room, two bedrooms, and a narrow galley kitchen, enjoys dramatic lighting conditions thanks to the complex spatial relationship between the gable of the exterior envelope and the gables of the interior spaces: the smaller scale of the interior gable structures creates interstitial spaces between the interior roofs and the exterior envelope. These interstitial spaces filter light from generous skylights in the larger exterior roof down to thin, translucent wooden sheets composing the ceilings of the living room and bedrooms. In the kitchen, an aperture telescopes directly up to the skylight of the exterior roof, providing copious direct natural light from above in spectacular fashion. Additionally, the space between the ceiling of the guest bedroom and the exterior roof accommodates a staircase leading up to a boxlike viewing platform.

While the house's exterior finish is galvanized corrugated metal sheeting that merely approximates the appearance of wood siding, inside the main living space and kitchen are distinguished by being finished entirely in warm maple panels, a material that extends to the translucent ceiling of the living room, which is composed of ultra-thin maple sheets. The result is a simple volume concealing a surprising array of interior spaces with complex qualities of light and shadow modulated by sunlight and trees.

Sections

Opposite: Though the House in a Forest resembles a child's idea of what a house should look like, the house's exterior form belies a complex arrangement of interior spaces, each with its own gabled ceiling.

Right: The smaller scale of the gable structures creates an intricate series of interstitial spaces between the interior roofs and the exterior envelope.

The structural complexity derived from the house's multiple gabled ceilings provides a variety of spectacular lighting conditions: in the kitchen, an aperture telescopes directly up to the skylight of the exterior roof, while the translucent ceiling of the living room is composed of ultrathin maple sheets.

Previous pages: All of the interior spaces are finished maple panels whose warm quality is enhanced by natural light filtered through the thin maple ceiling panels.

Loblolly House

Loblolly House

KieranTimberlake
Taylors Island, Maryland
2006

Having recently been awarded the commission to design a new embassy building for the United States in London, Philadelphia-based KieranTimberlake, headed by Stephen Kieran and James Timberlake, is emerging as one of the most lauded American architecture firms of the early twenty-first century. Among the projects the firm has completed during the century's first decade that have generated widespread interest is the weekend house that Kieran designed for his own family in the Chesapeake Bay region of Maryland. The 2,200-square-foot house, named after the copious loblolly pines found on its four-acre site facing Chesapeake Bay, represents the fruit of Kieran's preoccupation with creating structures composed of ready-made components, a line of inquiry that saw the firm's Cellophane House constructed as part of the Museum of Modern Art's 2008 exhibition devoted to prefabricated residential design.

Ground floor

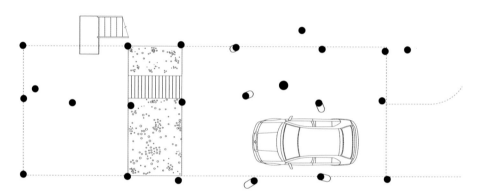

First floor

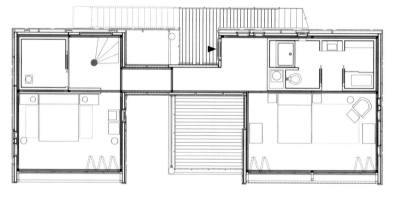

Second floor

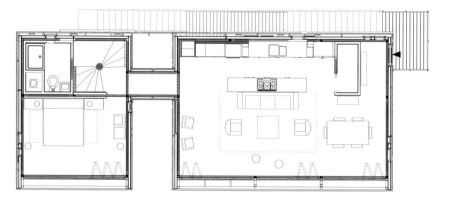

Loblolly House is raised a full level off the ground on timber piles irregularly spaced and in some cases driven into the ground at slight angles, emphasizing their relationship to the surrounding forest. Three of the four exterior walls further emphasize this relationship with their cladding in strips of red cedar, which are hung vertically to achieve a barklike effect. The house's fourth facade, facing the bay, is largely transparent, by contrast, thanks to two flexible layers of enclosure: first a layer of retractable hangar doors, and, behind these, walls of floor-to-ceiling glass panels that fold open like an accordion. The lower of the two living levels contains a large master bedroom and generous guest bedroom, each afforded maximum privacy thanks to a glass-enclosed corridor and the presence between the two rooms of an outdoor terrace covered by the overhang of the living room above. A spiral staircase ascends to the house's upper floor, leading to a large, open kitchen and living/dining space as well as an additional guest bedroom.

The relatively straightforward layout of the house's interior spaces is, perhaps ironically, a result of the house's somewhat unconventional method of construction. Easily assembled aluminum scaffolding supports floor and ceiling panels that the architects call "smart cartridges," which provide radiant heating, running water systems, ventilation, and electrical power. Bathrooms and other service elements were assembled off-site and simply lifted into place. This system of easy assembly, essentially by wrench, means that disassembly is equally simple, and that the materials composing houses constructed from such a system can be fully recycled rather than accounting for 40 percent of material in landfills, as is currently the case with conventional construction methods.

West elevation

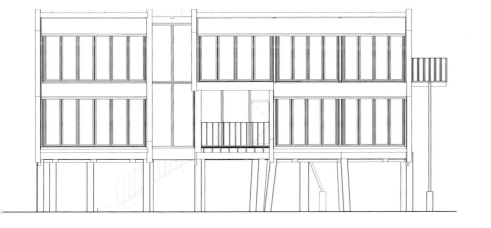

South elevation

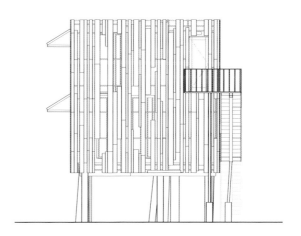

East elevation

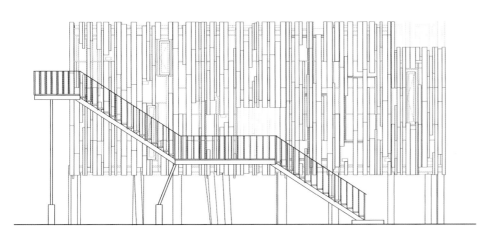

North elevation

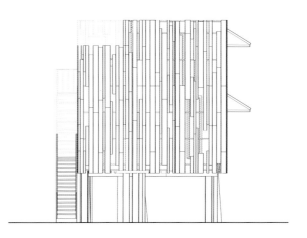

Left: Three of Loblolly House's four exterior facades are clad in barklike strips of red cedar.

Opposite: The house's water-facing facade is composed of two layers of enclosure: retractable hangar doors and floor-to-ceiling glass panels.

Following pages: By raising the house on timber piles, the architects have provided optimal views for all rooms on both living levels.

Archipelago House

Archipelago House

Tham & Videgård Arkitekter
Husarö, Sweden
2006

Up-and-coming Swedish firm Tham & Videgård Arkitekter, led by Bolle Tham and Martin Videgård, has designed a series of summer houses on islands in the Stockholm Archipelago. The most elegant of these, simply named Archipelago House, is constructed of fir plywood stained black to reflect the dark waters of the Baltic Sea, which it faces from its site on the island of Husarö.

Plan

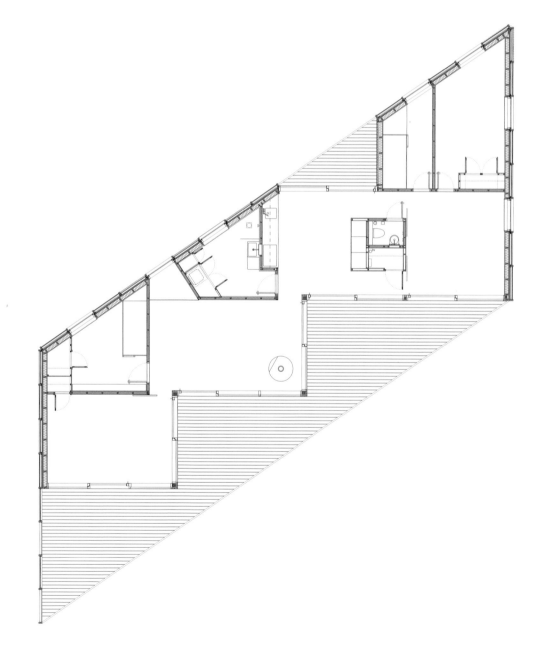

Comprising 1,400 square feet plus extensive outdoor terrace space, the house includes a large living room and master bedroom, both oriented so that they have floor-to-ceiling glass walls that face south and west. These two spaces, as well as a kitchen and a relatively large studio space, are staggered in zigzag fashion along the waterfront side of the house, while the rear facade is occupied by the bathroom and three small bunkrooms.

The unusual geometry of the house's plan is determined by the site, where the house is slipped into the level ground between two large rock formations at the water's edge. By lining the smaller rooms along the inland-facing side of the house, the house's more public areas, as well as the spacious master bedroom, compose a platform fragmented by expanses of glass opening onto the terrace, where protected outdoor spaces are nestled into corners formed by the saw-toothed edge of the house.

Elevation

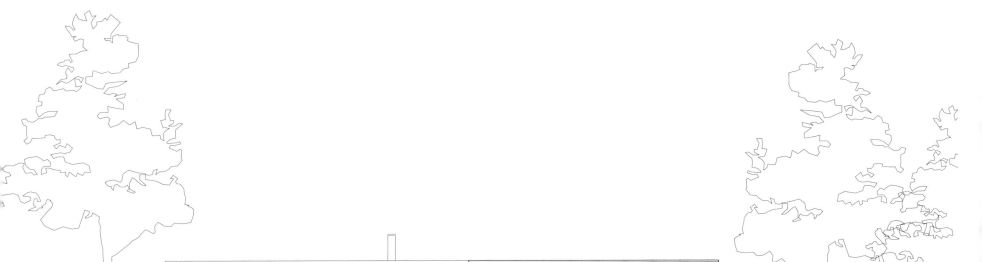

Opposite: Archipelago House is constructed of fir plywood stained black to reflect the dark waters of the Black Sea beyond it.

Above: The large living room and master bedroom have floor-to-ceiling glass walls that face south and west.

Previous pages: All of the house's waterfront-facing rooms—living room, master bedroom, kitchen, and a relatively large studio space—open to an expansive terrace.

Above and opposite, top: The living room and master bedroom as well as the kitchen and studio space are staggered in zigzag fashion along the waterfront side of the house.

Opposite, bottom: One of three small bunkrooms occupying the house's rear facade.

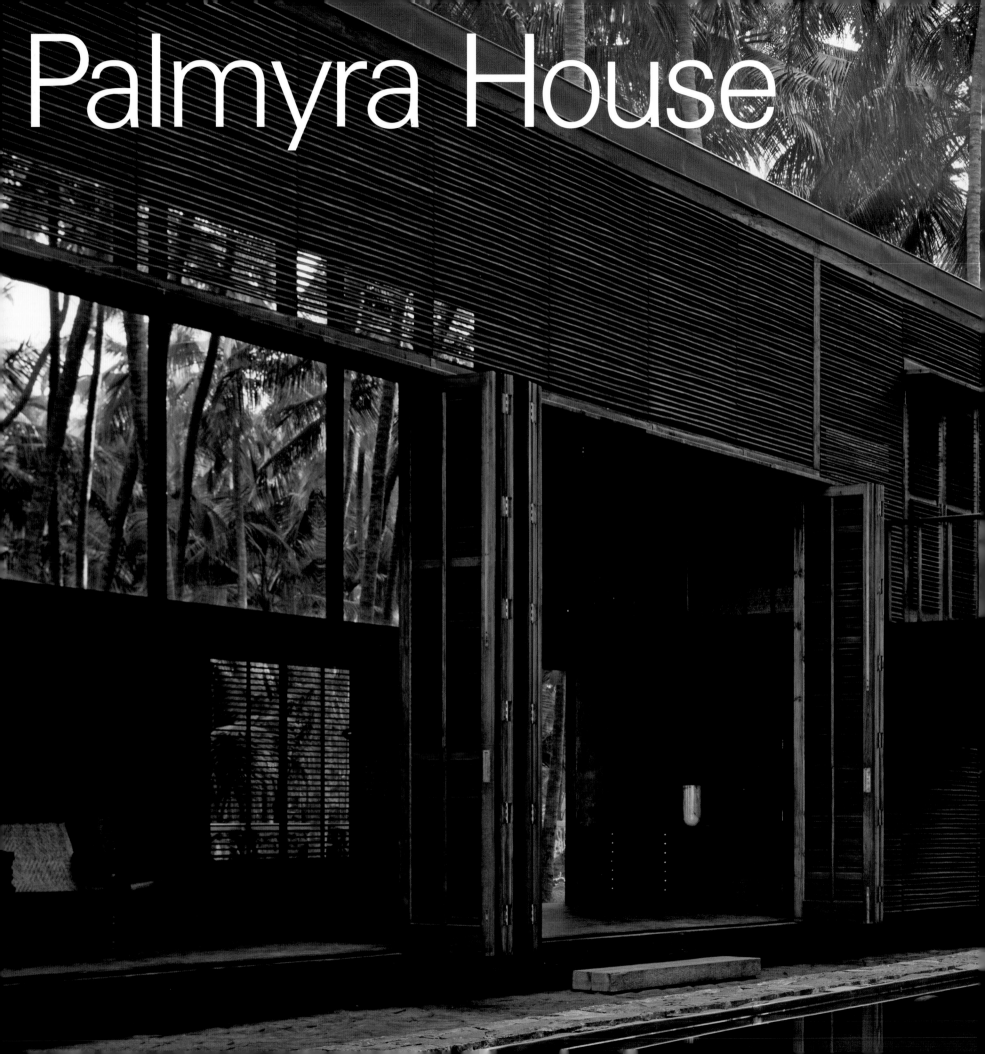

Palmyra House

Palmyra House

Studio Mumbai
Nandagaon, India
2007

For architect Bijoy Jain of Studio Mumbai, the Palmyra House was an opportunity to employ local, sustainable materials to construct a three-thousand-square-foot weekend house for a family based in Mumbai, about an hour away from the house's site on a working coconut plantation. Working alongside a team of carpenters with whom he has long collaborated, Jain prefabricated the house's structural elements for later assembly on site and investigated the possibilities inherent in a variety of finishes to create a structure that would harmoniously complement its unique site.

North block
Ground floor plan

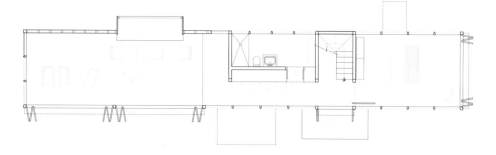

North block
Upper floor plan

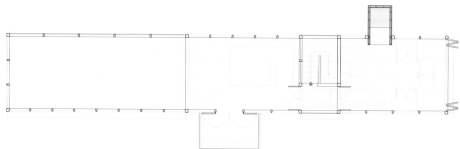

South block
Ground floor plan

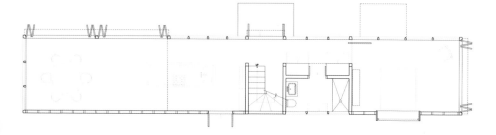

South block
Upper floor plan

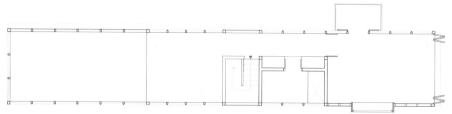

In fact, Palmyra House is composed of two structures, identically proportioned volumes set on a concrete plinth and straddling a twenty-five-foot-wide courtyard. The north volume contains a double-height living room and a study on its ground floor, and the master bedroom and large master bathroom on its upper floor. The south volume contains an open, double-height kitchen and dining space as well as a guest bedroom on its ground floor, with another guest bedroom and a sitting room on its upper floor.

The volumes' structural frames are composed of a local hardwood called ain, while the abundant louvers that give the house its decidedly porous quality were crafted from the wood of the palmyra trees that lend the house its name. Inside the house's volumes, framework of teak and walls and floors finished in pigmented cement plaster give the simple, rationally organized and open spaces a timeless, almost organic quality.

North block
South elevation

North block
North elevation

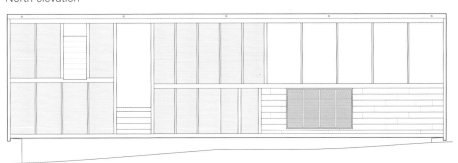

South block
North elevation

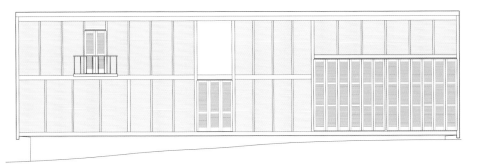

South block
South elevation

Opposite: The Palmyra House is composed
of two volumes straddling a courtyard
and pool.

Right: The extensive wooden louvers that
distinguish both volumes are crafted from
the wood of the palmyra trees that give
the house its name.

Top left: The copious louvered doors can be alternately opened and closed to provide varying degrees of shade to the interior spaces.

Bottom left: The master bedroom, on the upper floor of the house's north volume, overlooks both the living room and, from a small terrace at left, the courtyard and pool.

Opposite: Teak framework and pigmented cement plaster walls and floors give the house's interior spaces a timeless, organic quality.

Following pages: The extreme permeability of the house and its dependence on natural ventilation is demonstrated by its lanternlike quality at night.

Glenburn House

Glenburn House

Sean Godsell
Glenburn, Victoria, Australia
2007

Australian architect Sean Godsell has made it his ongoing project to adapt the vernacular architecture of his native land to create a sustainable design philosophy suited for building in the twenty-first century. This has resulted in a portfolio of strikingly forward-looking projects that rely on a set of time-tested strategies for negotiating the extreme antipodean climate. This particular essay is a couple of hours northeast of Melbourne in the rolling foothills of the Yarra Valley on a hillside site immediately adjacent to a national forest. The house is set partially within the hill, which provides significant insulation from the punishing heat of summer, as well as protection from harsh weather conditions during the rest of the year.

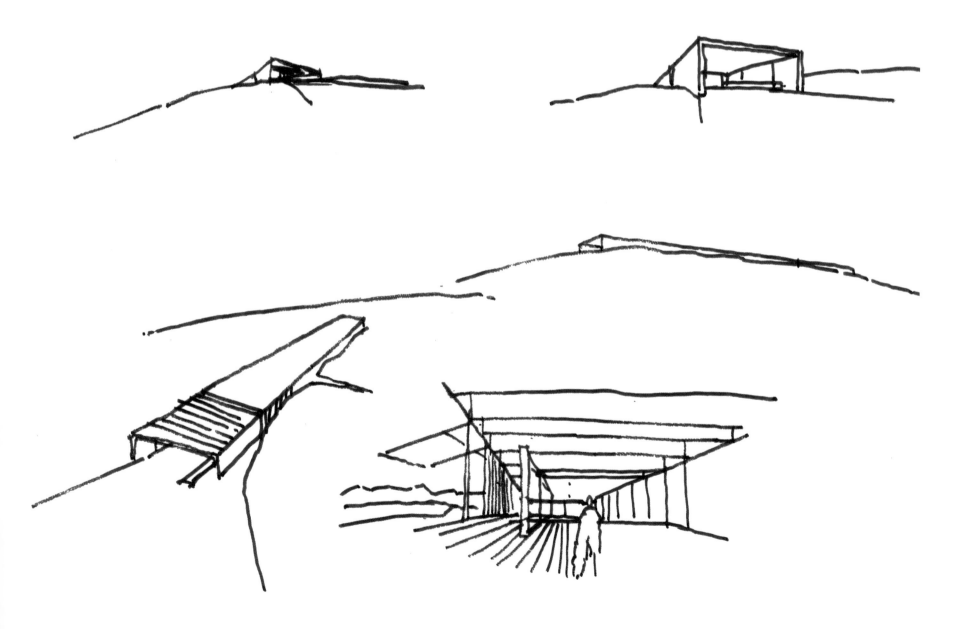

The long, box-shaped form is accessed at its center via an entry portal that leads to an enclosed deck separating the bedrooms from the main living areas, which along with the kitchen occupy a large, open space that leads to yet another enclosed deck and onto a carport. This relatively simple, linear arrangement of spaces is sheathed in a protective "skin" of oxidized steel grating intended for industrial flooring. The grated skin is divided into panels that pivot open to act as a classic modernist *brise-soleil*, offering protection from the sun while allowing air to move through the house. When fully closed, the grated panels take on an armorial aspect, giving the house a hermetic, monolithic profile.

The house's unique external structure, a signature of Godsell's most recent residential projects, also accommodates solar panels that not only supply electrical power and hot water but also act as a shading structure over the two deck spaces. Other sustainable features—such as double-paned coated glazing (rare in this part of the world), rainwater harvesting, and the digital optimization of power use by way of sensors in the floor slab's hydronic heating system—make the Glenburn House a highly effective machine for energy conservation.

Plan

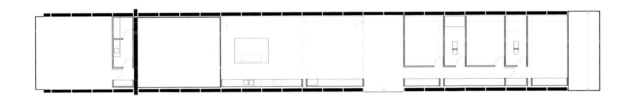

Elevations

Glenburn House is sheathed in a protective "skin" of oxidized steel grating that offers protection from the sun while allowing air to move through the house.

Opposite: The house is accessed at its center by way of an enclosed deck.

Right: The living room and kitchen occupy a large, open space.

The bedrooms are separated from the living spaces by the central deck and offer sweeping views of the rolling foothills of the Yarra Valley, outside Melbourne.

Dancing Trees, Singing Birds

Dancing Trees, Singing Birds

Hiroshi Nakamura & NAP Architects
Tokyo, Japan
2007

In the heart of Tokyo's bustling Shibuya Ward, architect Hiroshi Nakamura, who formerly worked in the office of Kengo Kuma, has created a sylvan, six-unit apartment building poetically called Dancing Trees, Singing Birds, the result of a competition held by the building's developer. Among those architects who participated in the competition, only Nakamura made conservation of the trees on the heavily wooded site a priority, going so far as to consult a tree doctor to determine how best to build on the site without damaging the trees' roots.

First floor

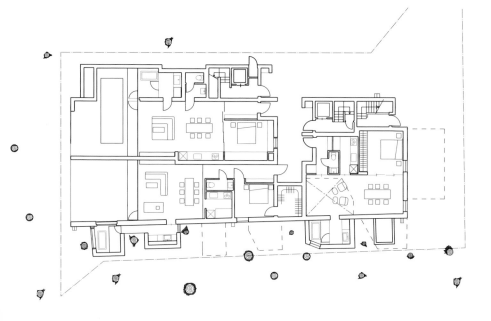

Second floor

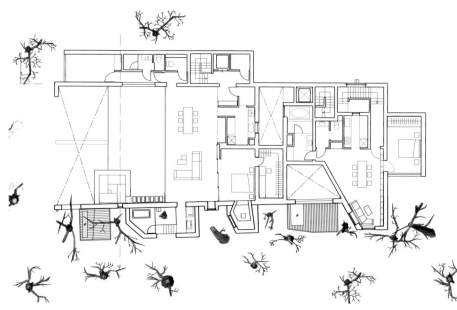

Terrace floor

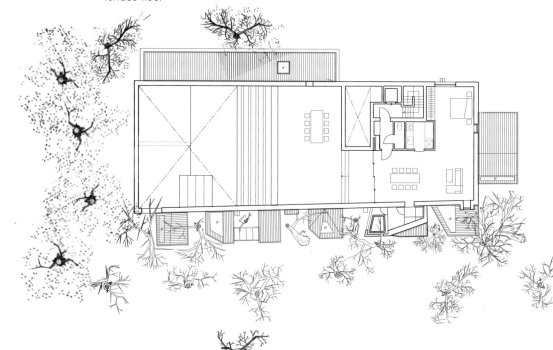

Nakamura's plan for the building called for the construction of a series of linked wood-clad "huts," to use Nakamura's term, which fit together in a freeform arrangement that favors the preservation of the building's site rather than the creation of an iconic structure with a strong formal profile. The result is a collection of building forms that appear to be half-hidden among the ever-present trees.

If the building's exterior maintains a modest profile, the individual apartments are flamboyantly expressive inside, with each one designed according to a theme, including a "Library House," in which every room is lined with books, and a "Tea House," which features a freestanding traditional tatami room cantilevered over an expansive reflecting pool. Each unit contains an open living and dining space, a bedroom, a kitchen, and a bathroom, as well as space dedicated to the apartment's respective theme. Additionally, Nakamura punctuated the building's southeast facade with compact, cantilevered structures, accommodating such amenities as a bath or small study—human-scaled echoes of the birdhouses Nakamura has placed among the structure's nooks and crannies to maximize one's sense of being enclosed within a forest in a world apart from the city.

Longitudinal section

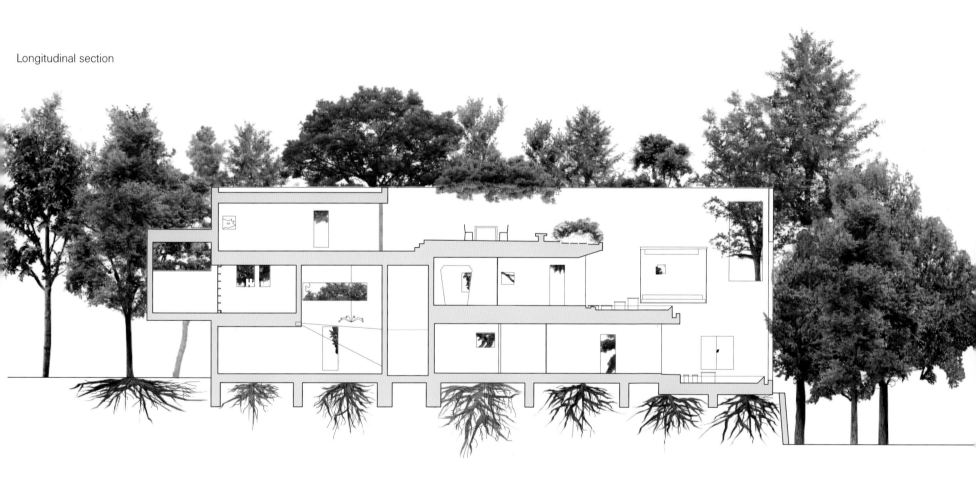

Previous pages: Though it is located in the heart of Tokyo, this six-unit complex is delicately sited among and around a heavily wooded site.

Opposite: The glass-enclosed staircase to a sleek wood-paneled tub room wraps around one of the trees on the site.

Right: A wood-paneled, skylit study occupies one of the small niches extruded from the house's facade.

Each apartment is designed according to a theme, including a "Pool House" (top left), a "Library House" (bottom left), and a "Tea House" (opposite).

Following pages: The Tea House features a traditional tatami room cantilevered over a reflecting pool as well as a framed view of the forest beyond.

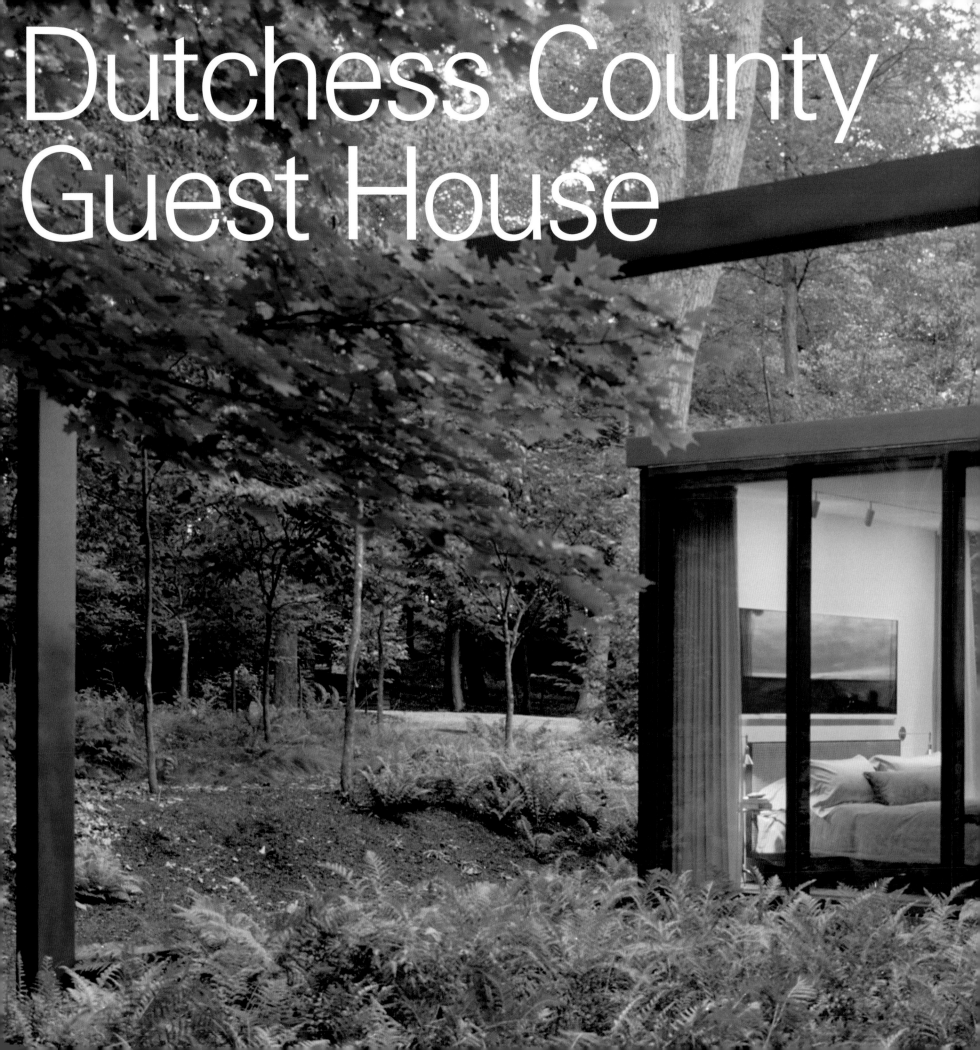

Dutchess County Guest House

Dutchess County
Guest House

Allied Works Architecture
Dutchess County, New York
2008

This small but highly polished guest house in Dutchess County, New York, in the Hudson River Valley just north of Manhattan, was conceived as part of a compound for a pair of art collectors that will eventually include a gallery and main house, also designed by Brad Cloepfil of Allied Works Architecture. Based in Portland, Oregon, and acclaimed for their Portland headquarters for advertising agency Weiden & Kennedy, Allied Works executed this 1,300-square-foot project from its New York office, where the architects tackled their clients' brief to create a retreat that would give guests close proximity to their larger weekend house while also providing a great deal of privacy.

Plan

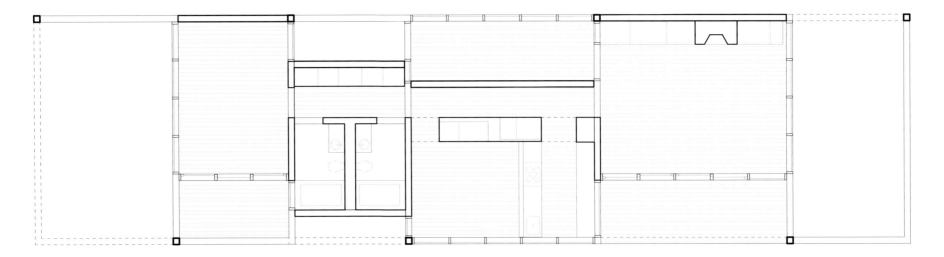

Cloepfil and his associates sited the house within a mature grove of trees so that the house's two bedrooms and main living space face a creek that winds through the clients' 350 acres. The project's great formal gesture, however, surrounds the volumes composing the house in the form of a slender steel-tube frame that delineates a simple rectangular volume within which the more complex arrangement of spatial volumes is realized. Within this frame is an alternating series of glass and mahogany panels, with the mahogany cladding extended to the house's flat roof, which will be visible from the couple's main weekend house.

Though small in scale, the house is richly detailed with mahogany cabinets and window mullions as well as slate and mahogany floors, all of which add to the sense of refinement and tranquility that are entirely appropriate for clients with a robust appreciation for fine art, as is the lyrical presentation of views achieved by the house's elegant steel frame.

West elevation

East elevation

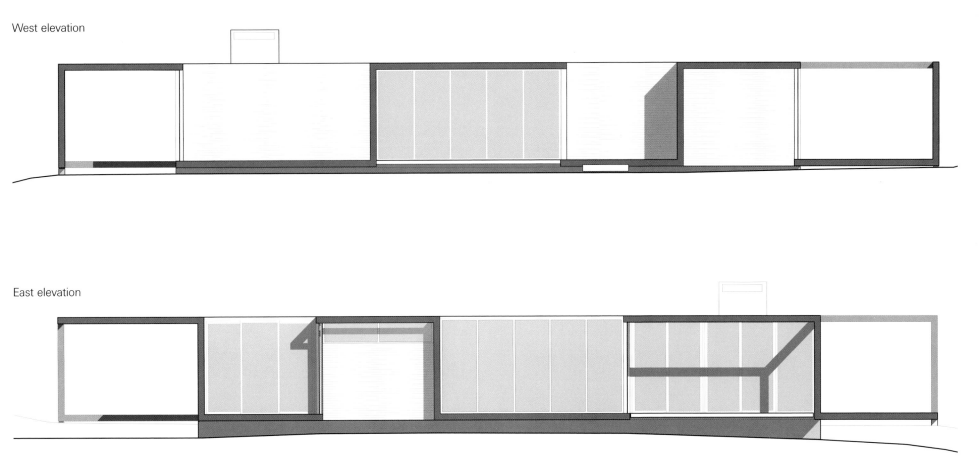

Brad Cloepfil of Allied Works Architecture set this 1,300-square-foot guest house in a grove of trees within its 350-acre site to meet his clients' request for a retreat for guests that would offer privacy while remaining close to the main house.

Opposite: The guest house's interior spaces were designed to accommodate pieces from the clients' extensive art collection.

Top right: The living room is richly detailed with mahogany window mullions and slate floors.

Bottom right: The kitchen features mahogany cabinets and floors.

This weekend house's most distinctive feature is the slender steel-tube frame that delineates a simple rectangular volume around the more complex collection of volumes that compose the house.

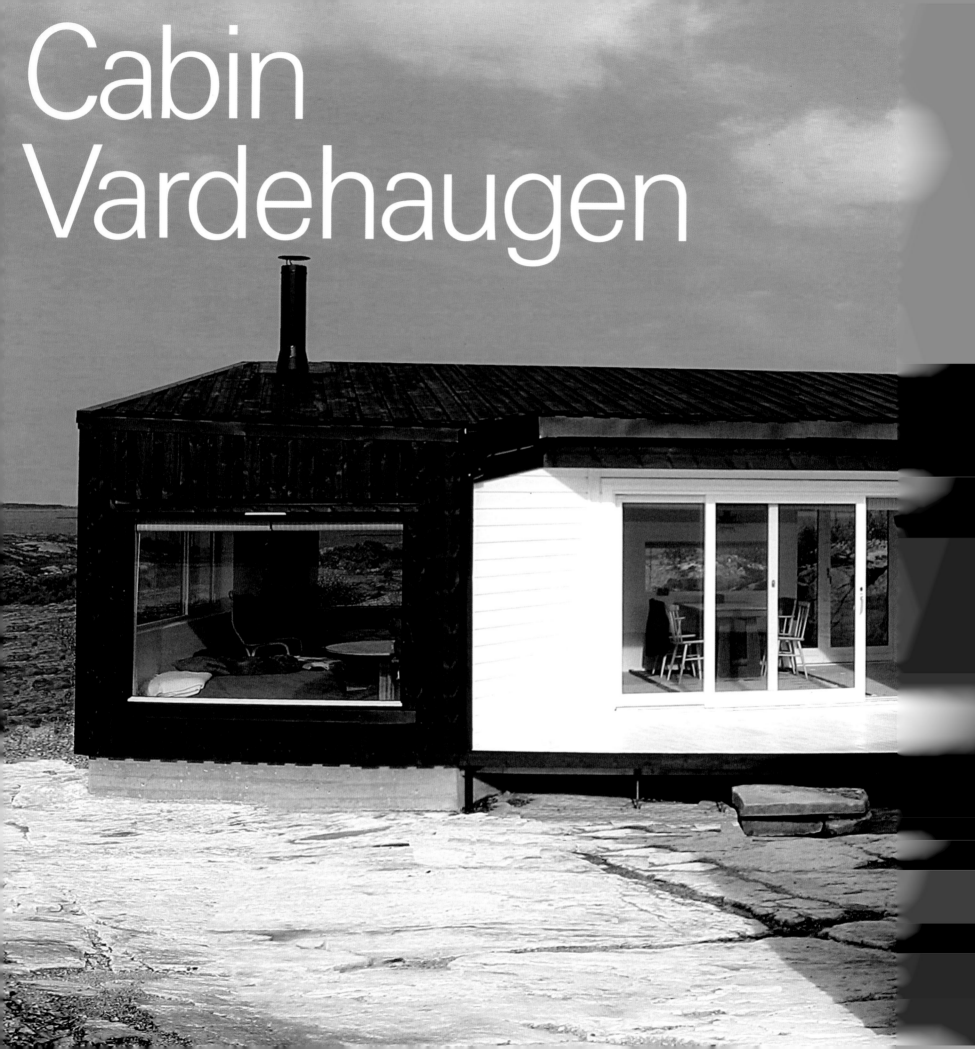

Cabin
Vardehaugen

Cabin Vardehaugen

Fantatic Norway
Grøttingen, Norway
2008

Named after the rugged outcropping atop the fjord on Norway's Fosen peninsula on which it is sited, Cabin Vardehaugen derives from traditional Norwegian "cluster structures," to use a phrase coined by architects Håkon Matre Aasarød and Erlend Blakstad Haffner of the firm Fantastic Norway. Describing such traditional structures as places where "flexible outside space and a clear social organization are the leading architectural principles," Aasarød and Haffner designed a two-bedroom cabin and an adjacent bedroom annex between which emerges an informal outdoor "atrium" that is sheltered by the two structures.

Plan

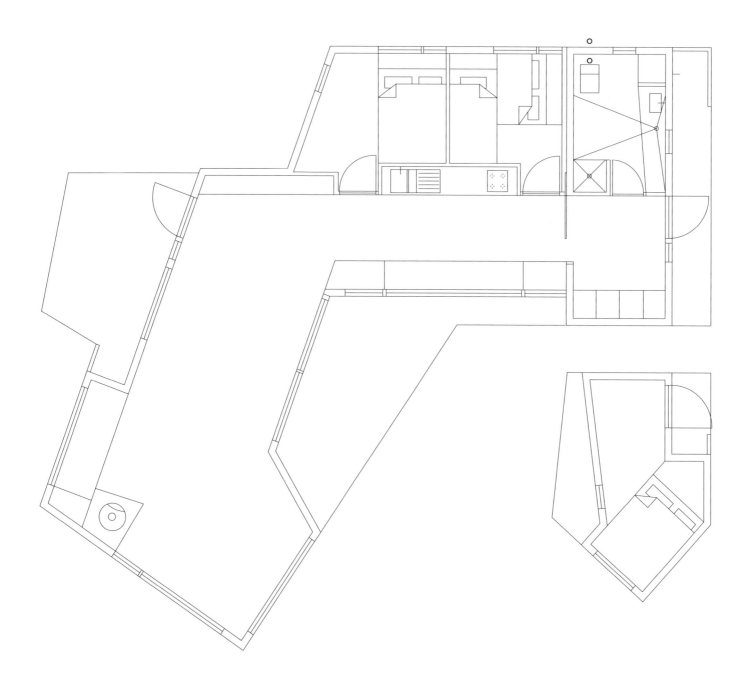

The architects developed the design over the course of a year of trips to the remote peninsula in order to observe the extremes in weather in the region and to consult with local authorities and residents on the design's progress, going so far as to outline the floor plan's various iterations in the snow at full scale.

The architects compare the cabin to a mountain fox curled up to shelter itself against the cold. Walls have been angled to minimize access to strong winds, and the roof folds down over wall surfaces at the cabin's most exposed points. The simple wooden structure of pressure-treated, water-resistant wood is anchored by steel rods that extend from the ground plane down to bedrock. Inside, the kitchen forms a spine between the bedrooms and bathroom, which face the heath on Vardehaugen, and the living room, which has a 180-degree view of the sea, allowing inhabitants to watch the path of the midnight sun from a transparent yet warm vantage point.

Section details

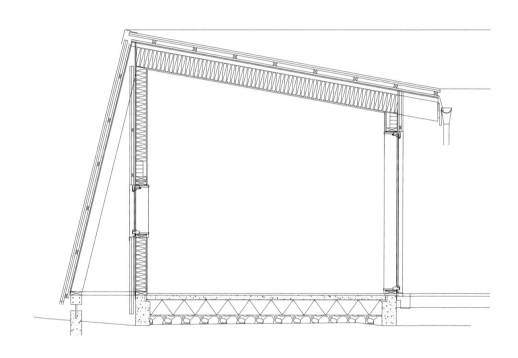

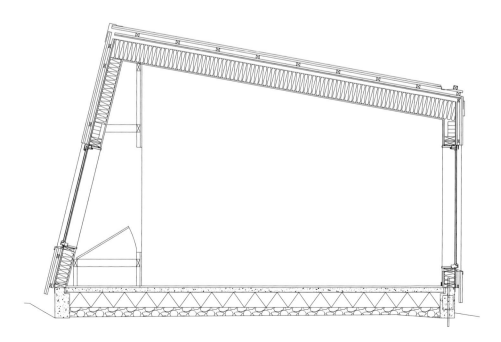

Angling Cabin Vardehaugen's walls and folding the roof over its most exposed surfaces, architects Håkon Matre Aasarød and Erlend Blakstad Haffner of the firm Fantastic Norway compare the cabin to a mountain fox curled up to shelter itself against the cold.

Following pages: The generous large-plate glazing in the living room provides a 180-degree view of the sea.

Opposite: Throughout the house, views of the surrounding landscape have been carefully selected and framed.

Above: The kitchen and dining area function as a spine between the living room and the bedrooms.

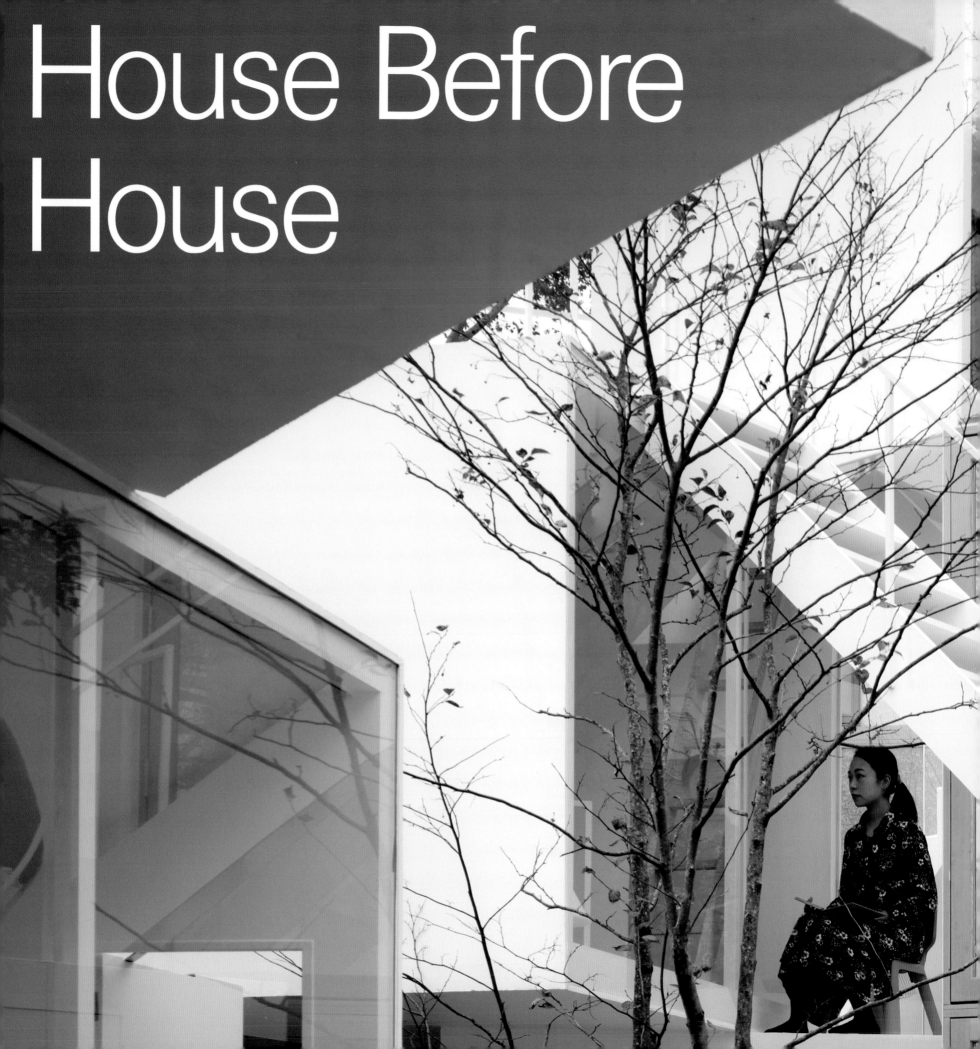

House Before
House

House Before House

Sou Fujimoto
Utsunomiya, Japan
2008

Unlike his 7/2 House, which is largely an exercise in formal and material playfulness, Sou Fujimoto's House Before House is a theoretical tour de force. Here, on an urban site in Utsunomiya, approximately sixty miles north of Tokyo, Fujimoto riffs on a series of dichotomies: between domesticity and wilderness, a technology-driven future and the primitive past, community and atomization. Divided among ten small cubic boxes, the house's 660 total square feet comprise a central living room, a kitchen, three bedrooms, a bathroom, a study, a storage shed, and a couple of ancillary spaces that provide nooks for hiding away, as well as ample outdoor living spaces, both on the ground and on elevated platforms.

First floor

Second floor

Third floor

Among the cacophonous organization of these boxes and platforms, Fujimoto also introduced a host of trees whose random arrangement within and on top of the house's various structures was intended to evoke a natural formation, such as a mountain, or an organically generated manmade phenomenon, such as a primitive village.

The house's extraordinary organization creates an entropic system that interrogates what Fujimoto calls the "commonplace yet precious totality of the act of living" by exploding the familiar functions of the single-family dwelling. Here all of the standard elements of the typical house—spaces for gathering, sleeping, cooking, bathing, etc.—are present, though their relationships to one another and to the surrounding urban context have been reconstituted to a revolutionary degree. Rooms are accessed via steep crisscrossing staircases or by traversing elevated ramps and bridges; their simplicity of form and provocative degree of transparency give the house the character of a futuristic cave dwelling, where daily life is an ever-renewable opportunity for discovery and adventure.

North elevation

Section

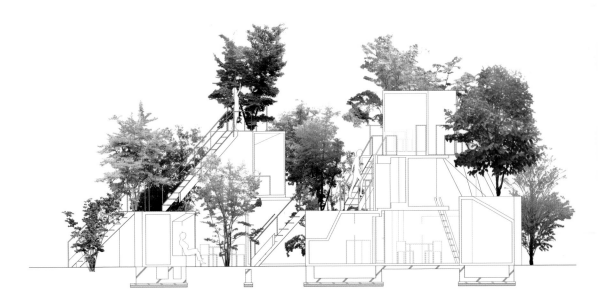

The 660 square feet of living space that compose House Before House are divided among ten small cubic boxes.

Opposite: Rooms are accessed via steep crisscrossing staircases or by traversing elevated ramps and bridges.

Opposite and bottom right: The rooms'
simplicity of form as well as a provocative
degree of transparency give the house
the character of a futuristic cave dwelling.

Top right: Trees within and on top of the
house's various structures reinforce this
organic quality.

Shell House

Shell House

Kotaro Ide/Artechnics
Karuizawa, Japan
2008

Though the area in and around Karuizawa, in Nagano Prefecture, is a popular resort destination, the region's high humidity coupled with low seasonal temperatures offer some challenging building conditions. When Kotaro Ide with his firm Artechnics was charged with designing a weekend house in the region, his immediate instinct was to create a sculptural intervention that would simultaneously give access to and protection from its lush forest setting. Starting with a large fir tree near the center of the site, Ide arranged the house so that all the living spaces look onto a circular terrace surrounding the fir. The terrace and therefore all the house's living spaces—including an open kitchen and living and dining space, four bedrooms, and a small study—have a view of a row of pine trees.

First floor

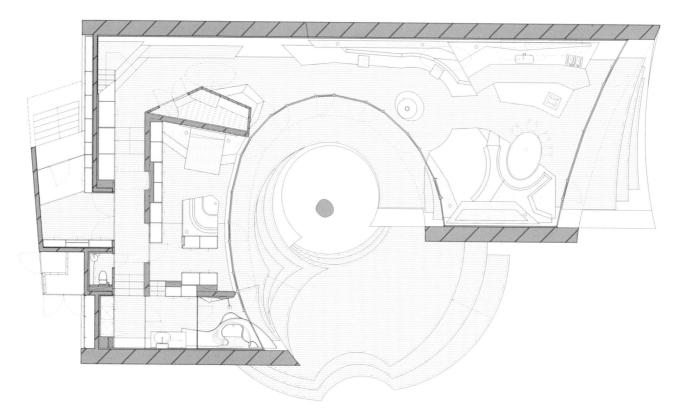

Second floor

Ide's second instinct was to counter this open, if already highly controlled, relationship to the house's natural surroundings with a strong structural gesture that would give the house a high degree of protection from the elements. The result is a bold structure composed of a concrete shell that envelops the living spaces and takes on a womblike warmth thanks to the generous use of wood for flooring and partitions. Additionally the floor is the source of indoor heating, minimizing energy consumption and acting as a cold-draft blocking system that allows the expanses of glass that distinguish the interior contours of the house's dramatic frame.

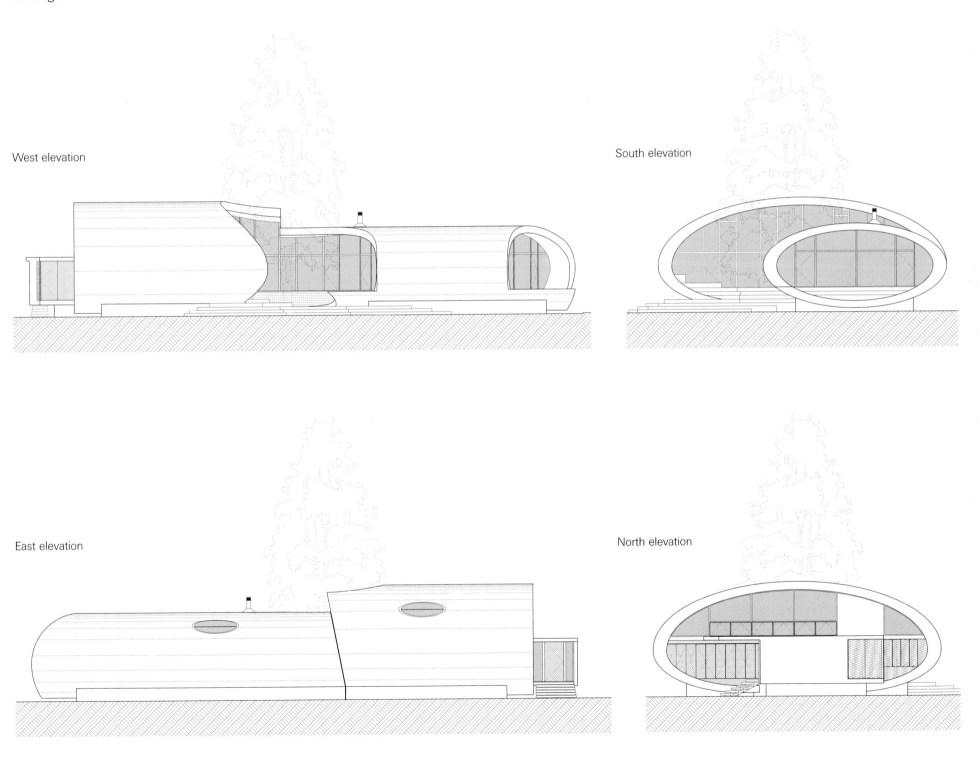

West elevation

South elevation

East elevation

North elevation

Architect Kotaro Ide designed the Shell House so that all of the living spaces look onto a circular terrace surrounding a large fir tree near the center of the house's site.

Though the house maintains a strong sculptural profile, its interior spaces maintain an immediate relationship to the central outdoor terrace.

Following pages: The house's boldly sculptural concrete shell envelops the living spaces and takes on a womblike warmth thanks to the generous use of wood for flooring and partitions.

Underfloor heating acts as a cold-draft blocking system allowing the expanses of glass that distinguish the contours of the house's dramatic frame.

Farm House

Farm House

Jarmund Vigsnæs
Toten, Norway
2008

This 1,600-square-foot weekend house for two academics and their family shares its site with a nineteenth-century farmhouse and barn that the clients inherited. Rather than rehabilitate the house and barn for their own use, the clients decided that a new construction would be more practical and that their dilapidated, uninsulated old farmhouse could be salvaged as quarters for summer guests.
The barn, however, was deemed a total loss, though architects Einar Jarmund and Håken Vigsnæs recycled much of the century-old barn's wood for the exterior cladding and terraces of the new house, providing the project with an underlying formal principle of radical adaptive reuse.

Upper level

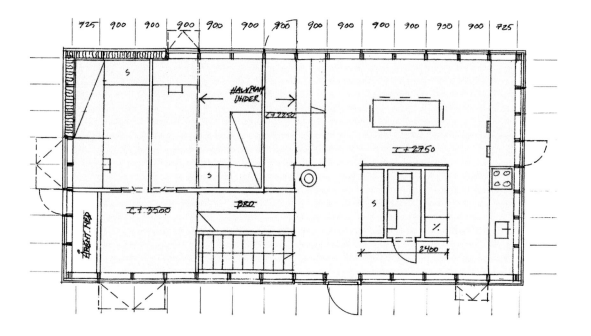

Lower level

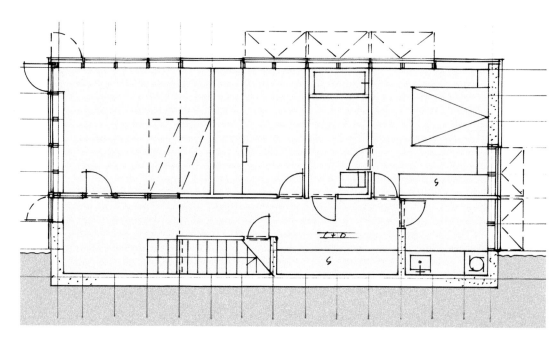

The house is simply and clearly organized on two levels. Its upper level comprises a long galley kitchen, an open living and dining space, and a loft with children's bedrooms. The lower level is dedicated to two bedrooms and a study. The house is oriented so the roof slopes upward toward the south with clerestory windows catching as much elusive winter light as possible, while the house's northern facade, with its expansive panels of glazing on both levels, transforms the dwelling into what the architects call a "winter garden" that operates as a solar heat collector. Together with underfloor radiant heating and a central wood-burning stove, these strategies make this revivified farmhouse a model of energy efficiency.

West elevation

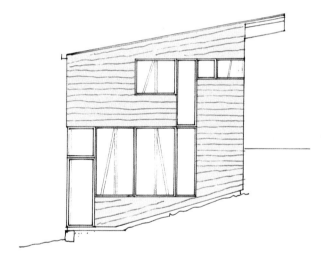

East elevation

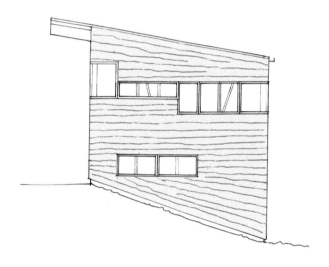

North elevation

South elevation

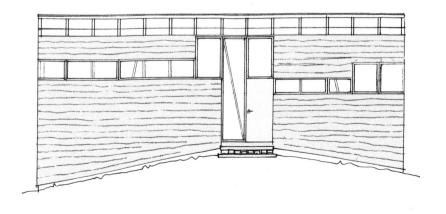

Left: Architects Einar Jarmund and Håkon Vigsnæs recycled wood from a century-old barn for the exterior cladding and terraces of this 1,600-square-foot weekend house.

Opposite: The house is sited at the edge of a large area of forest and overlooks one of the region's many lakes.

Opposite: The architects refer to the house as a "winter garden," with expansive glass panels on the northern facade operating as a solar heat collector.

Top right: The century-old wood planks enclose a state-of-the-art dwelling, demonstrated by the compact yet ample kitchen.

Bottom right: The generous use of plate glass and light wood panels gives all of the rooms an airy, spacious quality.

Kiltro House

Kiltro House

Supersudaka
Talca, Chile
2008

Architect Juan Pablo Corvalan, of the Chilean architectural design collective Supersudaka, named this elevated weekend house "Kiltro," the Chilean vernacular for "mongrel." The house is located near the city of Talca in Chile's fertile Central Valley, the region between the Chilean Coast Range of mountains and the Andes, on a challenging hillside site that demanded an ingenious solution. Corvalan made studies of a range of architectural precedents—international and local, contemporary and historical—which included projects by Le Corbusier, Mies van der Rohe, Rem Koolhaas, and countryman Smiljan Radic, whose Pite House is also featured in this volume.

Ground floor

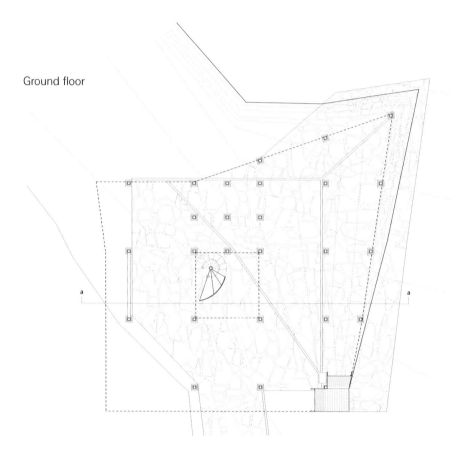

First floor

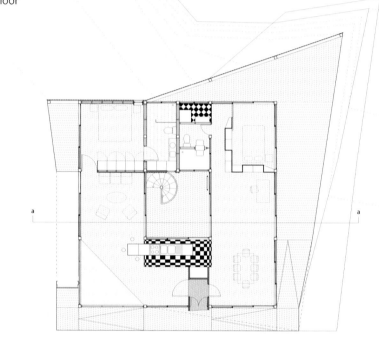

Roof terrace

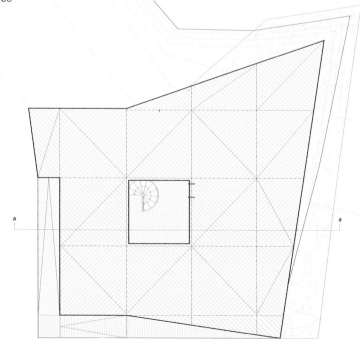

Combining these various concepts, Corvalan developed a hybrid solution that he has called "a bastardized design, like a crossbreed dog." Such a description is not inappropriate for a rough-and-ready project that responded not only to a challenging site but to a challenging budget as well. The plan was therefore developed out of a simple grid that belies the formal complexity of the house's structure, which takes the form of a faceted wooden envelope that extends down to create the exterior wall of the entrance facade, giving the structure an enigmatic, windowless profile. In fact, the roof appears as the house's primary facade from the site's downhill approach, with its undulating facets echoing the striking mountain landscape in the distance, and operates as a fully functional terrace accessed either by an external ramp or by a ladder down to a small, central atrium.

The house's wooden envelope conceals and distorts what is essentially a simple glass box set on *pilotis*. The orientation of the envelope offers protection from the sun during Chile's hot summer months, while the open glass facades and elevated floor plate allow passive ventilation and cooling. The interior spaces, arranged around the small atrium, are highly flexible, so that the living and dining spaces, which straddle an entrance vestibule and a freestanding kitchen island, can be alternated at will. Two bedrooms occupy fixed positions within the plan's grid, with the master bedroom enjoying access to a private terrace and the guest bedroom accessing a more public terrace. The exterior ramp wraps around the one-thousand-square-foot volume like a ribbon, offering access to the public terrace, the entrance vestibule, and the roof terrace, as well as dramatic opportunities for surveying the surrounding views.

Sections

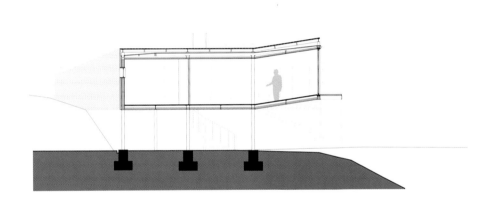

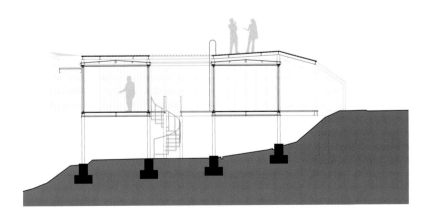

Left and opposite: Kiltro House is essentially a simple glass box set on *pilotis* open on three sides with views of the surrounding mountains through floor-to-ceiling glazing.

Following pages: The house's structure takes the form of a faceted wooden envelope that creates an enigmatic profile form on the entrance facade.

Left: The house's faceted roof echoes the surrounding mountains in the distance and operates as a fully functional terrace that can be accessed by a ladder down to a small atrium.

Opposite, top: An exterior ramp wrapping around three sides of the house also accesses the roof terrace.

Opposite, bottom: The atrium also offers access to the ground level via a spiral staircase.

Opposite: Inside the house, living and dining spaces are so flexible as to be interchangeable.

Right: The living and dining spaces straddle the atrium as well as a freestanding kitchen island.

Passage House

Passage House

TNA
Karuizawa, Japan
2008

Architects Makoto Takei and Chie Nabeshima of the firm TNA designed Passage House as part of the speculative development of architecturally ambitious weekend houses known as Owner's Hill in the Japanese resort town of Karuizawa. Facing a site that would require them to cantilever the house from a steep hillside, Takei and Nabeshima devised an ingenious structure that is ring-shaped in plan and partially embedded into the side of the hill in section. The submersion of one side of the house into the hill allows the structure to be freely cantilevered out above the steep ground plane rather than relying on support from *pilotis*; the ring-shaped plan enables the part of the house not embedded into the hill to be glazed on both sides, with elegantly curved glass panels following the curves of the striking construction.

Plan

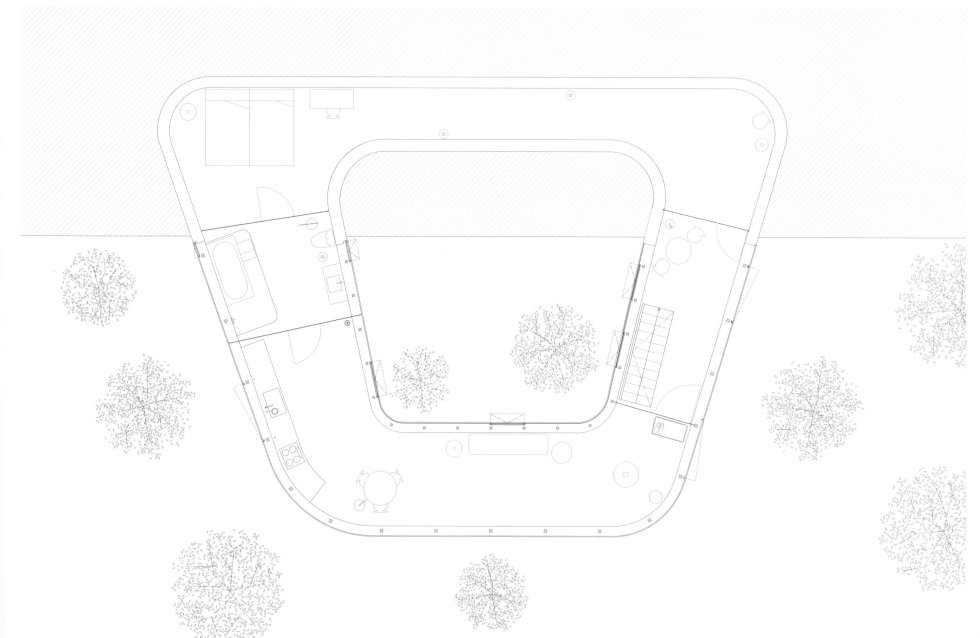

The house derives its name from the arrangement of interior spaces—including an open living and dining space, a kitchen, two bedrooms, a bathroom, and an enclosed terrace—along a circular continuum so that all the rooms serve collectively as a single path of circulation. Within that part of the house underneath the slope of the hillside, interior space is reduced to a dramatic, relatively narrow corridor.

Equally dramatic are the fully transparent floor-to-ceiling glass walls and doors that separate the rooms, including the bathroom, as well as the hatchlike entrance via a staircase tucked underneath the house and leading up to the enclosed terrace through a door set into the terrace's floor. The light-wood cladding on virtually all the interior surfaces softens the radical nature of the design, while the dark-stained wood exterior frame supporting the house's expansive ribbons of glazing helps to integrate this otherwise stupefying house into its idyllic site.

Section

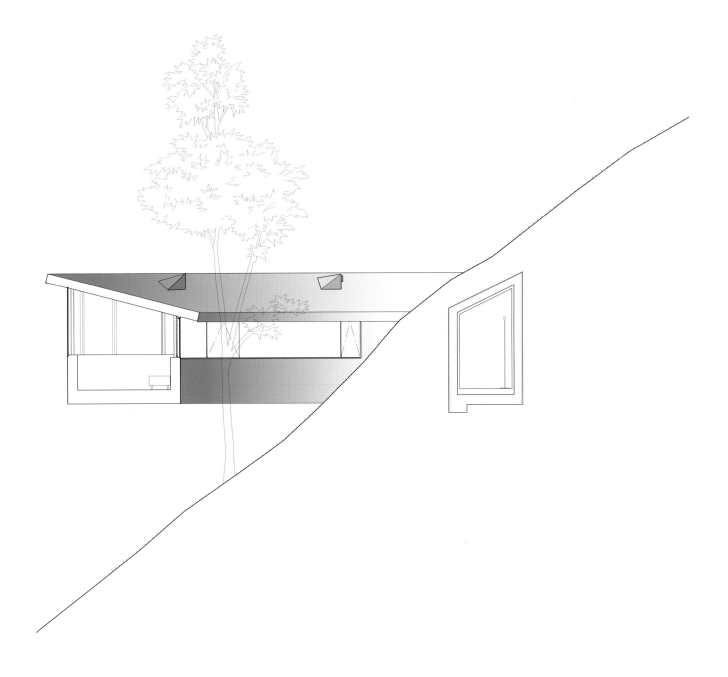

Facing a site that would require them to cantilever the house from a steep hillside, Makoto Takei and Chie Nabeshima of the firm TNA devised an ingenious structure that is ring-shaped in plan and partially embedded into the side of the hill in section.

Left: A hatchlike entrance via a staircase is tucked underneath the house and leads up to an enclosed terrace through a door set into the terrace's floor.

Opposite and pages 246–47: The house derives its name from the arrangement of interior spaces along a circular continuum so that all of the rooms serve collectively as a single path of circulation.

Pages 248–49: Within the part of the house underneath the slope of the hillside, interior space is reduced to a dramatic corridor that also serves as a gallery.

Bierings House

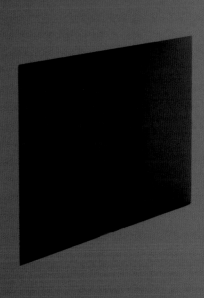

Bierings House

Rocha Tombal
Utrecht, Netherlands
2009

Although it is sited in a conventional suburban development outside of Utrecht, the Bierings House is distinguished by an ambitious use of wood on its exterior and an artful modulation of natural light in its interior. The simple gabled structure is composed entirely of narrow wood elements—even on its roof—that are punctuated by irregularly shaped, protruding apertures, all of which lend the house an expressive, highly sculptural quality. The seemingly random placement of these apertures reflects their function: to permit light and views to the interior spaces while minimizing any visual engagement with the surrounding banal built environment.

Ground floor

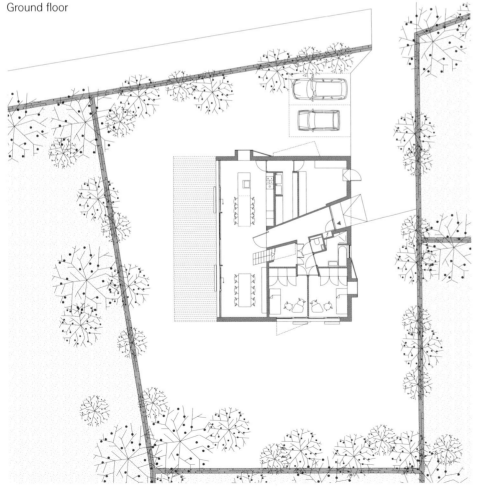

First floor

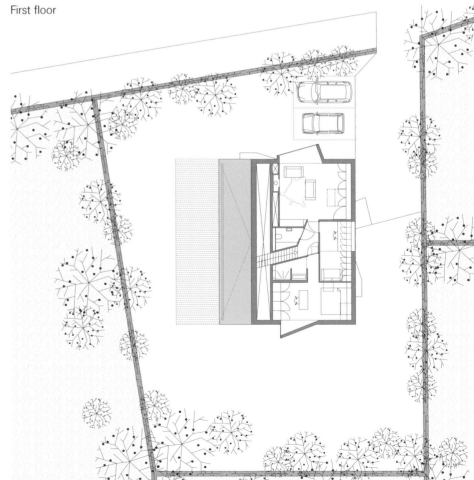

Inside, a telescoping entrance hall leads past two bedrooms to the kitchen and dining space, a long, open volume with a dramatic slanting ceiling and a garden-facing wall composed entirely of sliding glass panels, a striking contrast to the nearly blank entrance facade. Opposite this glass wall is a high wood-paneled wall that accommodates a large-scale pivoting wood door leading from the entry hall, the kitchen's work counter, a bank of bookshelves in the main dining space, and a narrow sculptural staircase that ascends along the same slanted axis as the entry hall.

The steep wood-paneled stair and wood-paneled upstairs hall give access to the main living space as well as the master bedroom and a small study, all finished in stark, white plaster. Here the apertures protruding on the house's exterior offer selective views and dramatic natural lighting conditions as well as a series of delightfully cockeyed nooks and dormers that give the austere spaces a whimsical, atticlike atmosphere.

Sections

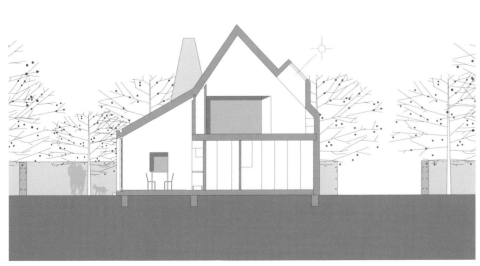

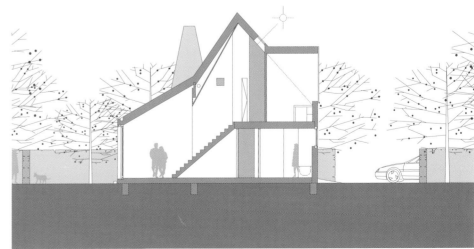

The simple gabled structure of the Bierings House is composed entirely of narrow wood elements—even on its roof—punctuated by irregularly shaped, protruding apertures, all of which lend the house an expressive, highly sculptural quality.

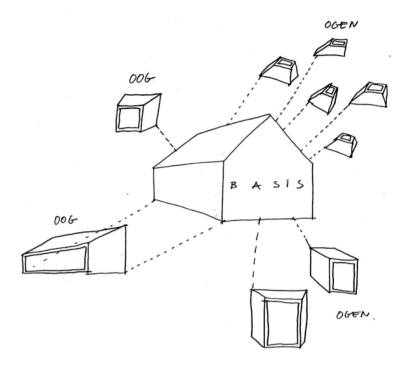

The house's lower level is dominated by a high wood-paneled wall that accommodates a large-scale pivoting wood door leading from the entry hall, the kitchen's work counter, a bank of bookshelves in the main dining space, and a narrow sculptural staircase that ascends along the same slanted axis as the entry hall.

Left: In the small second-floor study a desk occupies a niche within a dormer window, which nicely frames the view of the suburban townscape outside.

Opposite: On the upper level, in addition to the study, the living room and master bedroom also feature apertures that offer selective views and dramatic natural lighting conditions as well as a series of delightfully cockeyed nooks and dormers.

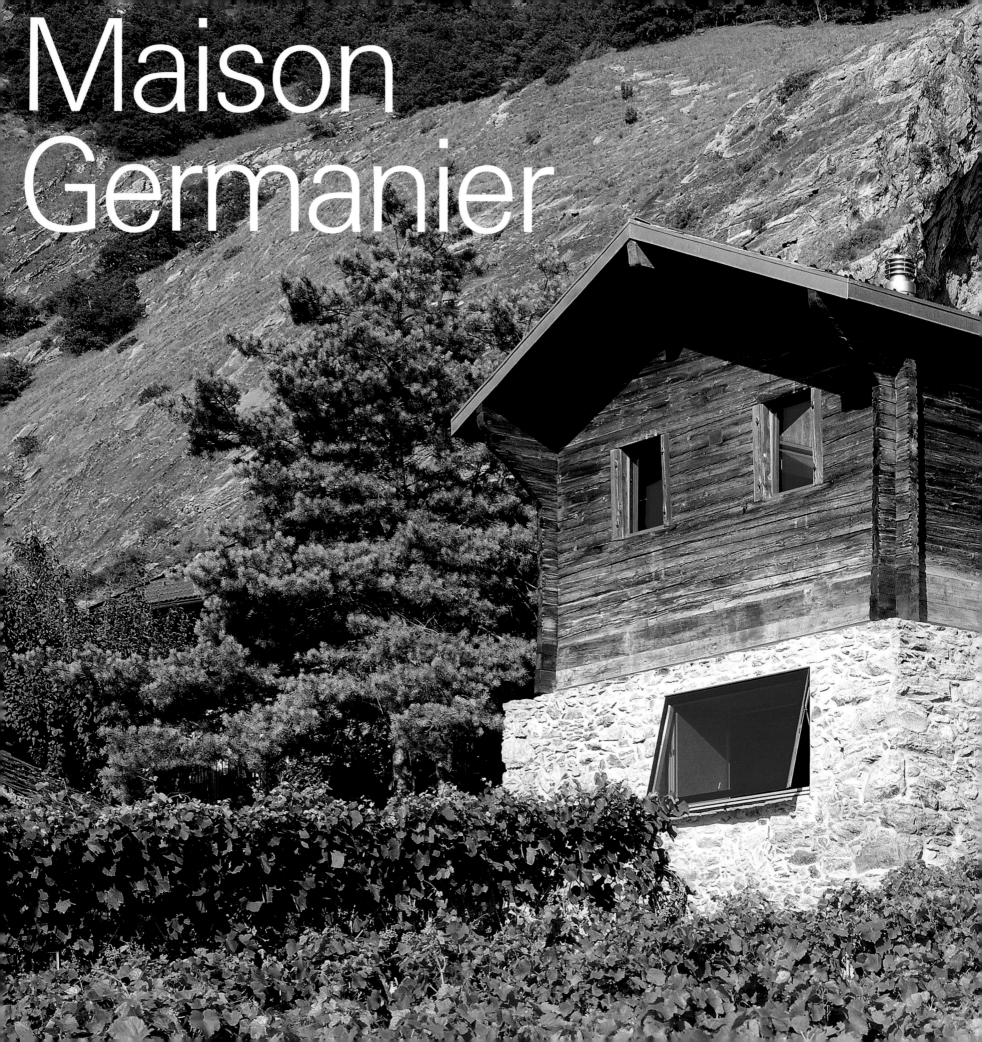

Maison
Germanier

Maison Germanier

Savioz Fabrizzi Architectes
Vétroz, Switzerland
2009

In the Swiss canton of Valais, noted for its ancient Amigne white grape cultivation, architects Laurent Savioz and Claude Fabrizzi were commissioned to renovate a house dating from the 1850s that served as the original winegrower's residence on this 170-acre vineyard. The architects satisfied the relatively straightforward program by arranging two bedrooms and a bathroom on the ground level and the living room and spacious kitchen and dining space on the house's upper level.

Second floor

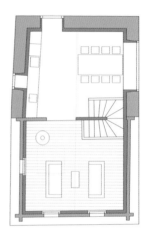

First floor

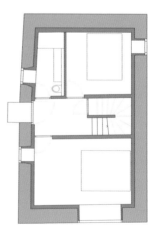

Basement

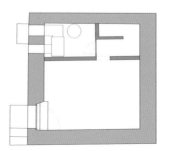

Sections

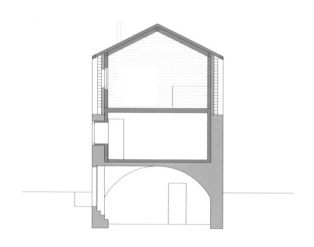

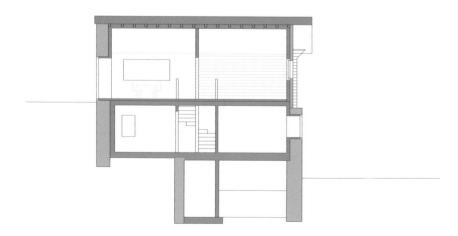

If the layout for the house is straightforward and perfectly appropriate in its antiquated shell, the materials employed within that shell are what make this project distinctive. From the exterior, the house maintains a highly traditional profile, at least at first glance. On the ground level, the rusticated walls are constructed of the same local stone that composes countless wine cellars in the region. However, apertures of sleek, single-plate glazing hint at a decidedly less traditional treatment for the house's interior. The stone construction is carried to the part of the house's upper level that contains the kitchen and dining area, while the adjacent living room is ensconced behind walls constructed of traditional wood planks.

This wood construction also constitutes the interior wall separating the living room from the kitchen, making the living space a sort of elevated cabin completely articulated in wood, including original planks of knotty larch on the floor—though its three interior perimeter walls are highly finished in contrast to the house's rough-hewn exterior. Polished exposed concrete floors and cement-coated panels on the ceilings and certain walls add yet another level of twenty-first-century refinement to this small-scaled yet ambitious example of adaptive reuse.

South elevation

North elevation

West elevation

East elevation

Opposite: This renovated house dating from the 1850s maintains a highly traditional exterior profile with rusticated walls constructed of local stone.

Right: A sculptural door, as well as sleek single-plate windows, hint at a less traditional interior within the stone and wood walls.

Left: Polished, exposed concrete treads on the staircase lead up to the second-floor kitchen and dining space, also featuring concrete floors.

Opposite, top: The bedrooms are clad in cement-coated panels.

Opposite, bottom: The kitchen, also featuring cement-coated wall panels, is a boldly contemporary space within the house's more than century-old shell.

Following pages: The kitchen's concrete floors add a twenty-first-century counterpoint to the rough-hewn wood walls and planks of knotty larch on the floor.

House in Moriyama

House in Moriyama

Makoto Tanijiri/Suppose Design Office
Nagoya, Japan
2009

Makoto Tanijiri faced a conundrum when commissioned to design a house on a narrow plot in Nagoya, Japan's fourth most populous city. Though the house's site was exceedingly compact, the client specifically requested a "garden room," handing the architect a somewhat unrealistic program for the design of a house on a site where even delivering adequate natural light would present a challenge. Tanijiri's inventive solution was to create a rock-filled garden space that occupies one perimeter side of the house and interrupts the circulation of space with pockets of vegetation.

Second floor

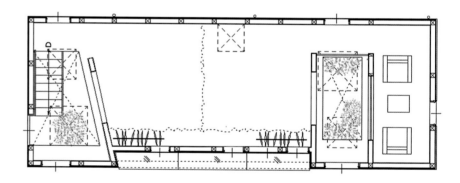

First floor

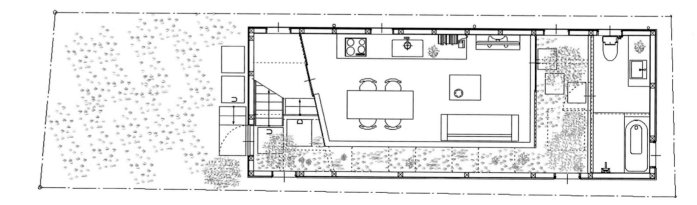

Entry to the house is accessed through a monumental double-height door on the otherwise blank front facade, leading directly into the garden space. Here two square stone treads lead to the stairs to the house's upper level as well as to two steps leading down to a door, nicely articulated in wood-framed glass, to the main room on the ground floor, a combination living/dining/kitchen space. This area is enclosed by expansive floor-to-ceiling glass panes along the edge of the garden space, creating a chamber within a structure. This fully transparent delimitation of interior and garden allows for the playful introduction of conventional interior elements—such as art or even furniture—into the narrow garden space.

Toward the back of the house the garden space punctuates the interior to create a point of division between the ground floor's main room and the house's single, amply proportioned bathroom. As in the house's entry sequence, stone treads pave the way through the garden space. And as in the garden space at the house's entry, the one here occupies a double-height pocket that allows natural light to filter down from skylights in the ceiling of the house's upper level and breaks up the single second-story sleeping and sitting area. In fact, because the exterior facades are minimally punctuated with small-scale square apertures, the entire house is virtually dependent on the natural light filtered from these skylights as well as from the top-lit gallery along the perimeter wall over the narrow interior garden.

Elevation looking east

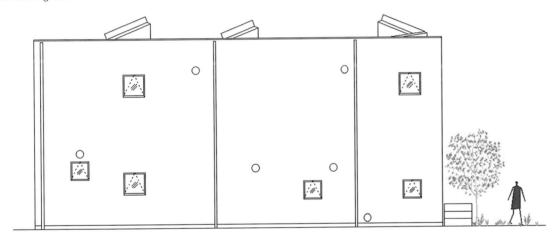
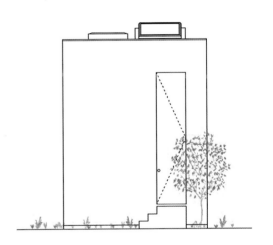

Sections

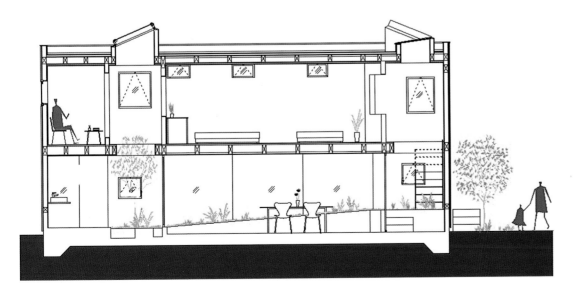
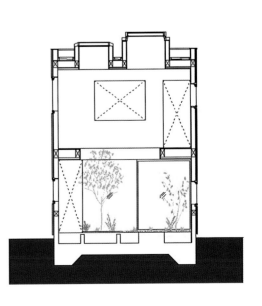

Top left: A monumental double-height door serves as the entry on the otherwise blank facade of the exceedingly narrow House in Moriyama.

Bottom left: The entrance leads directly to an interior garden space.

Opposite: The main room on the ground floor is enclosed by floor-to-ceiling glass panes along the edge of the surrounding interior garden.

Opposite: A double-height pocket of space allows natural light to filter from skylights down to both of the house's levels.

Right: The near absence of exterior windows makes the house dependent on these skylights as well as the top-lit gallery along the perimeter wall over the narrow interior garden.

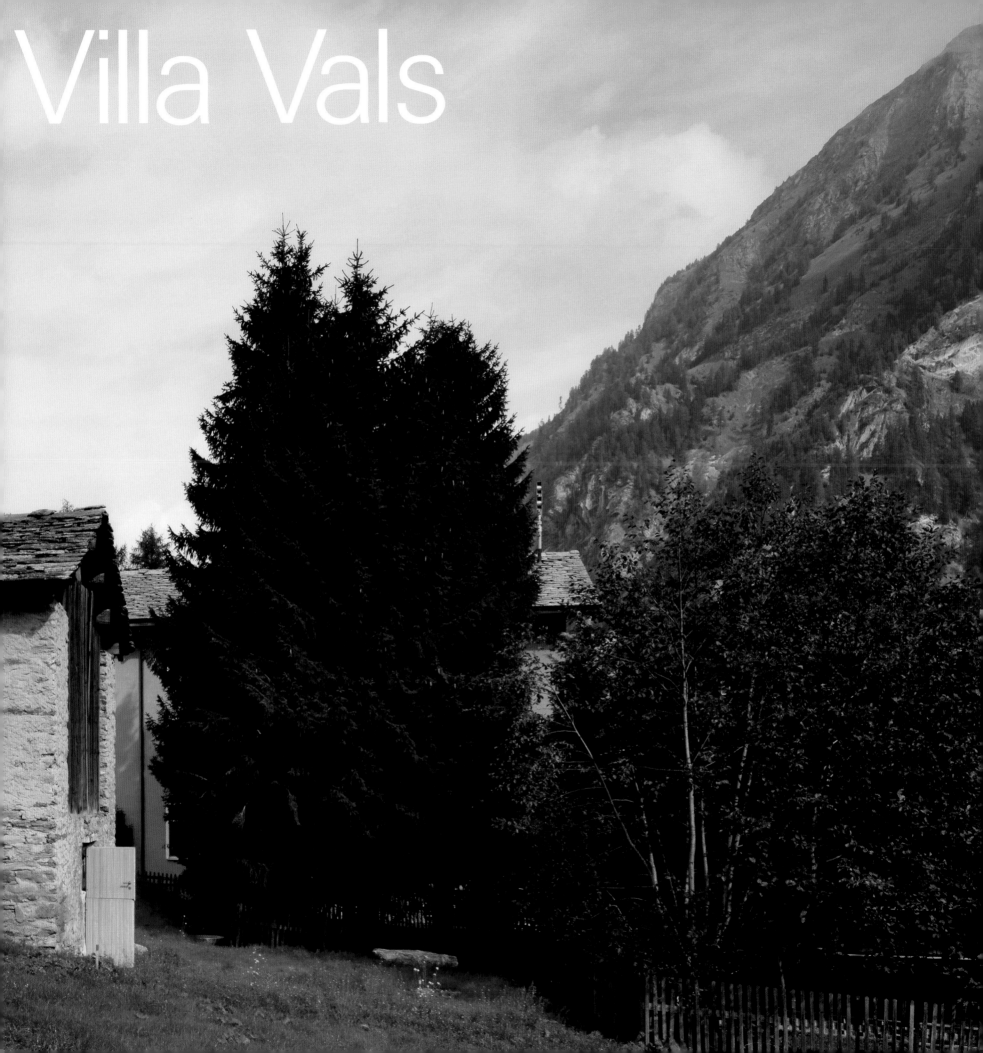

Villa Vals

Villa Vals

SeARCH/CMA
Vals, Switzerland
2009

It is ironic that such a bold design concept as the Villa Vals's was conceived out of deference to the adjacent spa designed by celebrated Swiss architect Peter Zumthor. Concealed within the side of a hill in Vals—an idyllic Alpine village with a population of fewer than one thousand and famed for its thermal baths—this collaboration between Dutch architect Bjarne Mastenbroek of the firm SeARCH and Swiss architect Christian Müller manages to maintain a remarkably distinctive formal profile while preserving the views from the baths and other neighboring buildings.

Site plan and first floor

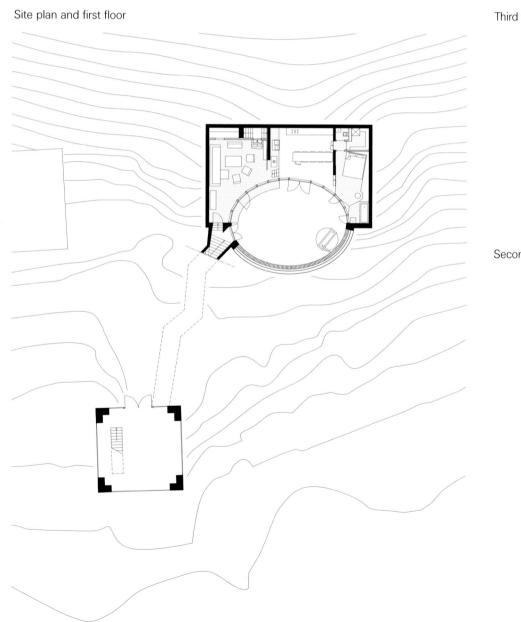

Third floor

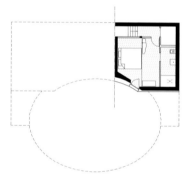

Second floor

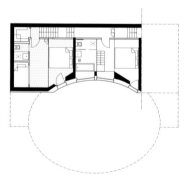

Entry to the eccentric structure is via an adjacent barn, which leads through a jagged concrete tunnel to a three-story, four-bedroom house completely embedded into its sloping site and arranged in semicircular fashion around an ovoid terrace. The large living room gives way to a sunken kitchen and dining room, which features a banquet-sized dining table. The variation in floor level between the living room and kitchen is characteristic of the entire house, which is a labyrinthine sequence of spaces tucked among a congeries of staircases and corridors.

The house's interior is a showcase for contemporary Dutch design, including sofas and lamps designed by Hella Jongerius, a whimsical outdoor bathtub on the terrace designed by Floris Schoonderbeek, and, in the master bedroom, Studio JVM's ingenious installation of cardboard shelves that extends up to the ceiling and across the room as a series of arches in the manner of a Gothic cathedral. All of these aesthetic flourishes obscure the fact that this singular structure is virtually energy neutral, thanks to triple-paned windows filled with krypton gas on the house's generously glazed, curved front facade, and radiant heating underneath the exposed concrete floors, and to the ambitious nature of its earth-sheltering concept.

Elevation

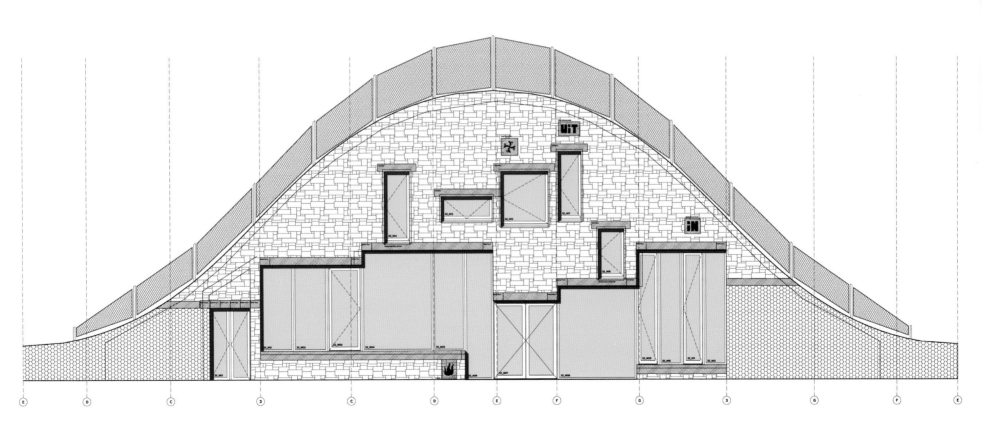

Opposite: This collaboration between Dutch architect Bjarne Mastenbroek of the firm SeARCH and Swiss architect Christian Müller is concealed within the side of a hill in Vals, an idyllic Alpine village with a population of fewer than one thousand.

Following pages: In addition to stunning views of the Alpine landscape, the terrace features a whimsical bathtub by Dutch designer Floris Schoonderbeek.

Opposite: The kitchen/dining room features a banquet-sized dining table.

Top right: Cardboard shelves in the master bedroom extend up to the ceiling and across the room like a series of arches in the manner of a Gothic cathedral.

Bottom right: The entire house features a dizzying variation in floor levels; here, in one of the second-floor bedrooms, a staircase not only leads to a window seat but also to a bathroom, at right.

Left: An adjacent barn serves as the house's main entrance, with access to the house proper through a jagged concrete tunnel.

Opposite: The concrete kitchen constitutes the same surface as the living-room floor.

Square House

Square House

TNA
Karuizawa, Japan
2009

While TNA's Square House is yet another project in the resort town of Karuizawa's ambitious Owner's Hill development, unlike the other Owner's Hill projects featured in this volume, it was not built on spec. Rather, architects Makoto Takei and Chie Nabeshima were commissioned by a couple to build a weekend retreat for them and their two dogs on the steeply sloping site they purchased in the neighborhood. Extremely narrow and located along the tree-lined ridge of a large hill, the site offered inspiration as well as challenges to the architects, who lifted the simple, glass-enclosed structure on elegant *pilotis*, which echo the bamboo and slender trees on the site.

Plan

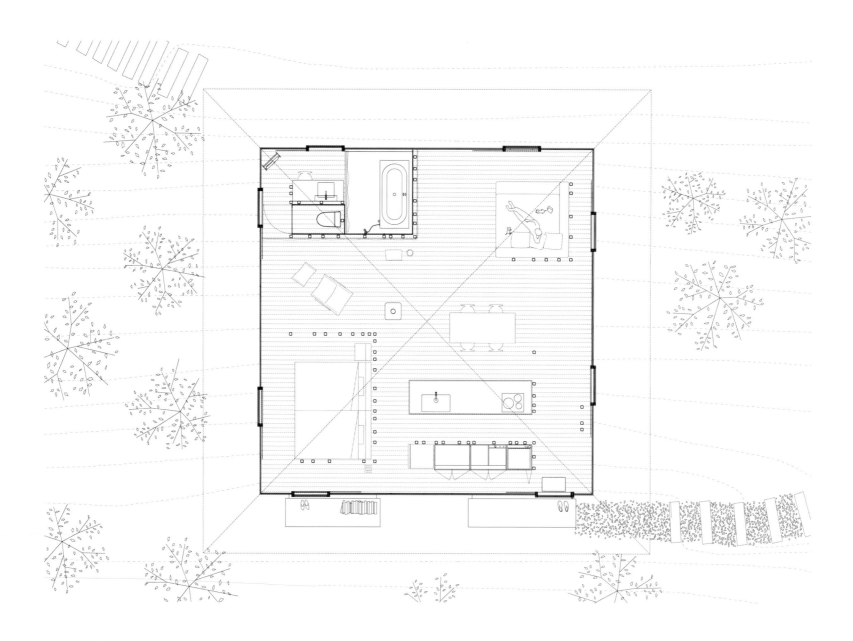

But instead of functioning merely as structural support in classically modernist fashion, these *pilotis* do double duty as delimiters of the house's interior spaces. Rather than spacing the supports evenly apart and fitting conventional walls within the resulting grid, Takei and Nabeshima arrayed them in linear clusters that span the distance between floor plate and ceiling to form something like walls, or shadows of walls to be more precise. The result is that the perfectly square plan is a loose organization of kitchen, dining, lounge, bedroom, and bathroom spaces, all equally open or closed to varying degrees, depending on one's immediate perspective.

The staggered intervals between *pilotis* in the house give the sense that slender trees occupy the interior spaces, while, in a complementary manner, the footprint made by the *pilotis* on the sloping ground plane seem arbitrary rather than rigidly dictated by a grid, so that the structural supports appear scattered around the site like the delicate forest they occupy.

Section

Opposite: The Square House's extremely narrow and steep site inspired the architects to lift the simple glass-enclosed structure on elegant *pilotis*, which echo the bamboo and slender trees on the site.

Right: The *pilotis* are carried through the floor plate into the house's interior.

The *pilotis* function not only as structural support but are also arrayed in linear clusters to loosely delineate the house's interior spaces, including dining and living spaces (top left) and the bedroom and bathroom (bottom left).

Opposite and following pages: Every interior space is enclosed within the house's four floor-to-ceiling glass perimeter walls, ensuring maximum transparency and openness to the surrounding forest.

Photography Credits

House in Bahia Azul Cristobal Palma

Mountain Chalet Hannes Henz

Great (Bamboo) Wall Satoshi Asakawa

Casa Rivo Cristobal Palma

Casa Poli Cristobal Palma

Pirihueico House Cristobal Palma

Izu House Edmund Sumner

House on the Rigi Valentin Jeck

Pite House Cristobal Palma

House in Brione Hannes Henz

7/2 House Daici Ano

House in a Forest Shinkenchiku-sha

Loblolly House Peter Aaron/ESTO: pp. 132–35. Barry Halkin: pp. 128–29

Archipelago House Åke E:son Lindman

Palmyra House Courtesy Studio Mumbai

Glenburn House Earl Carter: pp. 156–57, 160–64. Sean Godsell: p. 165

Dancing Trees, Singing Birds Daici Ano: pp. 166–67, 174 bottom, 175. Courtesy NAP: pp. 170–73, 174 top, 176–77

Dutchess County Guest House Hélène Binet: pp. 183–85, 186 top, 187. Jeremy Bitterman: pp. 182, 186 bottom. Dean Kaufman: pp. 178–79

Cabin Vardehaugen Håkon Matre Aasarød

House Before House Daici Ano

Shell House Nacasa & Partners Inc.

Farm House Nils Petter Dale

Kiltro House Cristobal Palma

Passage House Daici Ano

Bierings House Christian Richters

Maison Germanier Thomas Jantscher

House in Moriyama Courtesy Suppose Design Office

Villa Vals Iwan Baan

Square House Daici Ano